To:
Our Si...,
Phoebe,
Enjoy.
Stan & martha

MW01275370

998

The New Investors' Bible

Become wealthy
Starting at any age.

Stanton E. Christie

First Edition

Published by
WEALTH Incorporated, Seattle, WA

The New
Investors'
Bible

Become wealthy
Starting at any age.

© 1998 by Stanton E. Christie
First Edition
All Rights Reserved
Publisher's Cataloging-in-Publication
(Provided by Quality Books, Inc.)

Christie, Stanton E.
The new investors' bible : become wealthy starting at any age /
Stanton E. Christie. -- 1st ed.
p.cm.
Includes index & table of contents
LCCN: 98-90324
ISBN: 0-9664802-0-X
1. Investments--Handbooks, manuals, etc 2. Finance, Personal. 3.
Saving and thrift. I. Title
HG4527.C47 1998   332.6'78
                                                     QBI98-735

Published by WEALTH, Incorporated
1315 Madison Avenue, No. 5
Paperback   Seattle, WA 98104   Hard Cover
$19.95   Printed in the United States of America $23.95

ISBN 0-9664802-0-X

TABLE OF CONTENTS

Preparation

Preparation to becoming wealthy demands a new mental attitude
and the ability to change daily spending habits

Planning

Commitment

TABLE OF CONTENTS

CHRISTIAN FINANCE.COM

Thank you, Stan, for the production of such a fine book. This is just what was missing in the financial education areas. I refer, of course, to the WISDOM which only time and experience can give. You have done a fine service for us all.

The new generations of Christian investors, after reading The New Investors' Bible, can have the benefit of 50 years of wisdom, gained by a knowledgeable Christian in the active markets. This book, having been written without the bias that most books of this type show, gives the reader a feeling of at last getting the facts which truly empower them. Christian Finance.Com will feature exclusively the New Investors' Bible as our recommended background reading for all investors in all our communications.

Christian Finance.Com is to be placed on many search engines for the WWWEB which will result in interest for this book world wide. It is our goal to give your publication as wide an exposure as possible in this cyber environment.

G. Gordon Allen, CEO, Completion Corporation
Christian Finance.Com, Sponsored by Completion Ministries
Email C-CORP@ix.netcom.com

FOREWARD

Stanton Christie through 50 consecutive years of winning stock market transactions has expressed herein his mature belief, as in a religious faith, that within a moral certainty this book is a bible of conviction and a lifetime reference to act upon and to guide others to successful disciplines and practices when on the investment trail. These writings can be accepted for a lifetime as gospel for winning stock market doctrine.

An Iowa farm boy, he started investing at age four in an Iowa State bank which lost over $5,000 of his during the great depression era. Thereafter, he produced one million dollars three times in the stock market.

From a poor farm boy in his native Iowa to a successful businessman in Seattle, Washington, this gentle man, now in retirement, puts his mind to writing about stock market investments in order to share his wisdom, techniques, and practices with other investors, especially the young.

A composite summary of his investment know-how reveals herein how you can become wealthy, with sufficient income through your retirement years, to enjoy the better things in life.

The author shows that it really does not matter what your level of income is at the start. He states that the same principles and philosophies fit all who work regularly and can live within their means. The reader is admonished to set a goal and to stick with it for the remainder of his life.

The book also points out that even with a very limited start of only $30 per month, wealth can be made to grow fairly quickly. The mighty oak from a little acorn grows and grows.

FOREWARD

Regarding his investment philosophy, the author exhorts his readers to never have a long period of time with money lying idle. Further, he advises never buy into a company without full knowledge and information about it. To keep from having investment losses requires thorough research.

Authoritatively, this book discloses with easily understood language, how to work the market. It covers the logic of stocks, compounded mutual funds, transfers or roll-overs from mutual funds into money-market funds and timely reverses thereof with reasons why. Within certain practical commandments, he exhorts personal disciplines of the reader to enable early escape from loss during times of panic, or loss under pressure of media seduction to acts of greed.

The author turned market maven tells what to do and what not to do during a bull or bear market. He explains how to perform when a stock of yours splits, and how to diversify your portfolios.

He encourages critical record keeping and knowledgeable relationships with experienced fund brokers to research stock issues, pointing the way to bolster your long term retirement funds, for all the reasons you may have for them.

About the Author

I have had the pleasure of knowing Mr. Stan Christie for over 18 years. Stan has been a leader and over achiever since he was a young lad in school back in Belmond Township in North Central Iowa. He was an honor student and salutatorian in his senior class in High School of 50 graduates of 1934. After graduation, Stan went on to college during the great depression at Iowa State University. Stan put himself through school by doing odd jobs, waiting on tables at the Fraternity that he belonged to or any manual labor jobs that he could pick up.

Stan was also on the track and field with the University for three years! He held the world record for two years in the 440-yard dash and held the American record in the 220-yard dash for two months. Adding to his acclaim, he also held the Four-A state record in the 220-yard dash, which lasted for 19 years. Stan graduated as Salutatorian in his class in 1938 at Iowa State University. Later he received his PhD from Iowa State U.

Stan has tutored people and families over the years in investments and has written many books on investing in the market, which contributed to many of these folks in becoming very well to do, and/or millionaires!

Stan stands tall in my eyes as a person with high morals and business ethics and a person who never gives up. He has written several books on investing in the stock market and mutual funds, plus he's living a normal life, overcoming his handicaps caused by a severe stroke. Knowing Stan as well as I do with his ingenious wit and knowledge about investments and the stock market, these next several books cannot miss being Best Sellers. People who buy them and follow his guidelines cannot miss being successful!

Denny Lockett

About the Author

I have known Stanton Christie for over fifteen years. In my judgement he has an uncommon ability to extract difficult financial information and make it available to the lay person in a readable form.

Mary Jane Moffat, Author and Educator

My friend Stanton helped thousands of investors improve their income over the past forty years. In retirement for the past 18 years, he has conducted classes for thirty or more families quarterly and has taught young investors to use their skills effectively for long time returns. Stanton continuously sought to assist people of all ages with their investments.

In 1996, an executive with Fidelity Investments, a large Mutual Fund Company, proclaimed Stanton to be among the top 50 individual investors in American. He specializes in assisting young investors plan and implement their lifetime investment programs.

John Clemme

During the past decade when Stanton and I began our series of discussions about investing, it was evident that a priority in his life is a caring, sharing concern for the investment future of people surrounding him, for young, mature and older. He has almost an obsession for sharing his more than 50 years as a successful investor with others.

During succeeding years, he introduced us to the advantages of a relationship with a discount brokerage firm to enable us to add to our portfolio independently. Our diversification has greatly surpassed the growth that our assets would have had on the route we were on ten years previous.

About the Author

Stanton's writing of years past has recently been coalesced into his latest book, "The New Investors' Bible." His story is ever timely and potent. A good European friend has followed Stanton's investment advice through conversation and reading materials now available in "The New Investors' Bible." He is a satisfied investor and plans a special trip to the Pacific Northwest to share the good fortunes of global investing which Stanton influenced him to study and follow!

A Thankful Friend, Siegfried Kiemle

Retired School Teacher and Biological Consultant

Stanton E. Christie is a conservative broker and money manager in the investment market. He conducted business in his own office with his successful staff for 40 years in real estate and investment sales.

During his career, six of his clients thanked him for assisting them in becoming millionaires. Two have likewise so reported during Stan's retirement of 18 years. Many others raised their living standards and sent sons and daughters to college with investment earnings gained through Stan's guidance.

John Nuke

What Others Say

With a sterling record as a stock broker for 40 years, Mr. Christie has brought his keen vision and rare insights to bear on the world of investments with his book, The New Investors' Bible.

In clear, incisive prose he details steps you need to know to succeed as an investor, and he highlights practical ways, in dealing with extremes, to protect your investments during bull and bear markets.

Due to his investment skills many clients have said that his guidance led them to become millionaires.

You owe it to yourself and family to acquire this unparalleled guidepost to investing. It will be a most useful tool for years and years from now.

Peter Lindberg

It is indeed a tribute to speak on behalf of my long time friend, Stanton, who successfully led many investors to further their earnings over the years. Eight investor clients contacted him to express their appreciation of his advisory skills in aiding them to become millionaires. He guided hundreds over his 40 years as investment broker.

He has always stressed the importance of diversifying holdings extensively to reduce risk and research all recommended entities.

1996 was his lifetime high earnings. He was active in several Federal Income Tax exempt funds and his net earnings were strikingly impressive.

John G. Gollie

What Others Say

The investment market likely has more negative factors than positives to distract investors from earning large profits. Mr. Stan Christie has never experienced an investment loss. This is mainly because each entity is placed in his research file for three years as an artificial investment. If the entity fails to meet his high standards of earnings, it is discarded. Thus, his earnings have been high. That spells success in the investment market.

. Marian Hsu

Stanton Christie began his lessons in investments at age four on his family farm in Iowa when he saved a nickel instead of spending it. For years, he has continued to study all aspects of the financial scene. I followed his advice and was able to take a marvelous trip to Scandinavia on the profits from my investments. In a rapidly changing economic world, some verities remain unchanged and I do believe that Mr. Christie probably still is investing most of his nickels in the future instead of squandering them on items that will be gone tomorrow.

Mary Jane Moffat

My investments recommended by Stanton E. Christie have performed very well over the years. He is a keen student of the investment market and assists many investors regularly with their investment holdings. He has a host of friends scattered over a broad range of our nation. His most recent holding yielded 55.6% in 15 months. His retirement years appear to be equally as productive as were his professional years.

Doris Gabrielson

Acknowledgements

I have not tried to encompass in these credits all those friends who have contributed to my writing of this book. To attempt to do so would be another small book.

For those whom I perhaps should give credit, but have not, I ask forgiveness on the basis of so many years having passed since I began this undertaking, my memory fails me now.

Special credit must be acclaimed for my wife Martha for her secretarial skills and proofreading all contents of 21 books, each with a comprehensive index, graphs, tables and many articles which have supported this endeavor. To produce one articulate and rounded out treatise of information, to help others who engage their time and hopes in stock market transactions has been a labor of love for me.

I also want to credit the counselors Mary Jane Moffat, Siegfred Kiemle, Robert Kirk, Peter Lindberg, John Gollie, and John Clemme who offered guidance when needed, also contacting me frequently. All are cherished friends.

BIBLIOGRAPHY

Over the years, many publications have been referred to as sources of information and data for study and development for a wide assortment of subjects, including investments, used by the author as educational material.

The author has been an avid reader and student of technical and educational books, transcripts, articles, magazines, news articles, government reports and other miscellaneous reports and data. His ability to retain subject matter has been invaluable to him as a teacher and writer over these many years.

Some of the references that come to mind include: The Investor's Business Daily, the Seattle Post Intelligencer, "Made in America" by Peter Ueberoth, Rich Levin and Amy Quinn, Standard and Poor's Investor's Monthly, A Man's Right to Wealth, The Atlantic Monthly, U. S. News, The Seattle Times, and Fidelity Investments.

All investment procedures are discussed in The New Investors' Bible, together with acute timing reports and constant study of the general market and daily newspapers. These make up the guidelines for the writings, recommendations on investments and management of the author's personal portfolios.

PREFACE

This is a composite summary of investment experiences of the author over a 50 year period. It reveals how to become wealthy starting at any age, with sufficient income through retirement years to enjoy the better things in life.

Stanton E. Christie, the author, declares that it really does not matter what level of income one has. The same principles and philosophies fit all who work regularly and can live within their means.

Even with a very limited start, say $30 a month, we are reminded that the mighty oak tree from a little acorn grows and grows.

This book is truly about becoming wealthy, starting at any age. It gears readers with self confidence to understand investment market techniques and proven strategies that in some 40 years produced a million dollars three times for the author.

It discloses authoritative procedures within understandable perceptions of how to work the stock market. Discussing the logic of stocks, mutual funds compounded, money markets, and how bonds perform, it tells how to manage your funds in a bull market as well as a bear market. Certain commandments exhort the reader to exercise lifetime disciplines to escape loss during times of panic or greed motivated by media pundits, news headlines and electronic reports of today's market happenings, world wide.

Mr. Christie explains mutual funds and money market funds with uses for each and benefits peculiar to each. Detailed research of a company to find incorruptible research data for its investment potential is stressed as a must activity prior to any investment commitment. The book shows how.

DISCLAIMER

This book is written and published to provide information in regard to stock market investments and other securities, and how to manage investment portfolios, etc. It is sold with the understanding that the publisher and the author are not engaged in rendering legal, accounting, authorized investment or other professional services.

If specific investment, legal or other expert assistance is required, the services of competent professionals should be sought.

It is not the purpose of this book to act as a registered broker of securities nor to reprint all the information that is otherwise available to the reader, the author or the publisher.

For more information, see the many references available in the text and/or glossary of terms herein.

Every effort has been made to make this book as complete and as accurate as possible to help the reader to prepare himself, to plan his goals, and to commit to investment procedures that will make him wealthy in due course of time. There may be mistakes, both typographical and in content, therefore, this text should be used as a general guide and not as the ultimate source of writing or publishing on the subject matter.

The purpose of the book is to educate and to entertain. The author and WEALTH, Incorporated, shall have neither liability nor responsibility to any person or entity with respect to any loss or damage allegedly caused directly or indirectly by the information contained in this book. Regarding author's yields and successes, past performance is no guarantee of future results. Before you invest or send money to be invested, call for a prospectus and read it carefully.

MAKE EVERY DOLLAR COUNT

Most people today learned as youngsters to spend money as though it might go out of style. The American society lives an "easy come, easy go" way of life. Everyone seems always to be waiting for the almighty paycheck to spend.

Sensible and thrifty Americans who have security within their philosophies and way of life feel out of place with the helter-skelter neighbors down the block. Financially secure Americans always know that such people are looking for short-cuts and half-finished projects: Know that with a weak bank account, big bills and charge accounts, they probably never will get out of debt.

Thrifty people learned at a young age to live within their means by adjusting their habits and goals to a reasonable outlook. Wealthy people have climbed the corporate ladder or built a business into a successful venture. Most wealthy people have in common a relentless drive to accumulate capital. This attitude adjustment and the real facts behind creating wealth for yourself, are the main theme and objectives of this book.

It really does not matter what level of income one has. The same principles and philosophies fit all who work regularly and live within their means. There are dozens of ideas here to consider. Select the ones which apply to your liking and stick with them. Set your goals and keep them for the remainder of your life. The mighty oak from a little acorn grows.

GATHERING AND USING INFORMATION

Living rich requires you to make a commitment to change. Fortunately, this need not be a painful process! Small adjustments in the way you spend your money and the way you perceive the world around you can help you to start building wealth rapidly. In turn, this can lead to a better standard of living for you and for all of us. Prepare yourself mentally and accordingly.

This book is a mass of items assembled with subject

1

matter varied intentionally to keep the reader's interest and attention.

References used comprise a multitude, as from authorities and from common people scattered all around our great nation; most particularly the reference of common sense. The author began managing his money at age four as a poor farm boy, and through assiduous application of the practices referred to here, accumulated a mass of wealth three times. This made it possible for him to provide more than a million dollars for care services and medicines for each of three major illnesses to date.

This book will show you 81 ways to expand your assets and become more efficient in the things that are truly important. May you enjoy every day, and experience a long, wholesome way of living. Remember, the mighty oak tree from a little acorn grows.

BEGINNER INVESTORS AND MUTUAL FUNDS

Beginner investors have much to learn. The vast amount of material can be scary. The following choices of major considerations will save you years of research time and possibly considerable costs. For instance, I researched a dozen or more mutual fund companies and selected Fidelity Investments for many reasons. To list a few: Fidelity offers much helpful data for beginners as well as experienced investors. Their toll free telephone service is very helpful. They have a large assortment of mutual funds from which to select. A local office is convenient and staffed with knowledgeable personnel.

My choice of mutual fund categories was "Growth," Within the Growth segment was Contrafund, Magellan, Equity-Income II and Puritan. Soon I will subscribe for Fidelity Blue Chip Growth Fund. Its five-year earnings record is 18.93% annually; lifetime earnings are 19.57% annually. The fund's goals: Long-term capital appreciation by investing in blue chip companies of U.S. It has a 3% initial sales charge, and initial capital required is $2,500; for IRA and Keogh minimum investment is $500. The fund is devised for long-term (five or more years). It invests in companies that are at the top of their industries. Most recently, the fund invested in technology, finance, and energy sectors for their promising long-term growth potential. My plans include investing about $5,000 in the fund annually for many years in the future.

Fidelity Blue Chip Mutual Fund is designed for long-term growth. By leaving all dividends and capital gains distributions, the fund will yield maximum returns to the investor. He can expect the fund to double in value about every four years, considering a particular amount of holdings for the full term. Other data are explained in the prospectus. Contact them for more information.

In considering your financial goal, stock mutual funds can play a major role in helping you reach for your financial goal. Savings and earnings for a child's education or for retirement may be enhanced through investing in growth type mutual funds. Risk level is considered to be nominal. By investing in Fidelity Blue Chip Growth Fund, the investment expertise of the Fidelity team, which has been proven many times to be superior, will be working every business day for you. The fund is firmly rooted in Fidelity's belief that there is no substitute for in-depth, hands-on research when it comes to analyzing the growth potential of a company. A wide range of shareholder services are available to each mutual fund investor. Their toll free telephone services are available around the clock seven days every week.

DOUBLING YOUR MONEY: THE RULE OF 72

To estimate how long it'll take your money to double if you achieve a certain return, divide 72 by what you might earn. The result tells how many years it will take for an investment to double at a given rate, provided the earnings are allowed to compound.

If you put $100 in an account that pays 3% interest and don't add another penny, except the interest you're reinvesting, you'll have $200 after 24 years (72 ÷ 3 = 24).

That $100 will double in 7.2 years if it earns 10% (a figure that is illustrative of the long-term average annual return of stocks and not representing any fund). (72 ÷ 10 = 7.2.)

Interest Rate Earned	Years to Double Your Money
3%	24.0
4%	18.0
5%	14.4
6%	12.0
7%	10.2
8%	9.0
9%	8.0
10%	7.2
11%	6.5
12%	6.0
13%	5.5
14%	5.1
15%	4.8
16%	4.5
17%	4.2
18%	4.0
19%	3.8
20%	3.6

The Value of Starting Now

Monthly Investment	Number of Years to Reach Your Goal		
	5 Years	15 Years	25 Years
$500	$35,796	$158,481	$405,036
$750	$53,695	$237,722	$607,554
$1,000	$71,593	$316,962	$810,072

The chart shows the future value of different hypothetical monthly investments for various time periods, assuming an annual return of 7%. Example returns are pre-tax, reflect monthly compounding, and do not represent results of any periodic investment plan in any Fidelity fund. Different investments may perform better or worse than the rates shown in this chart, and principal value and return may vary.

From Fidelity Investments.

A research file must be considered one of your vital tools in your investment program. Subject titles should be carefully planned to permit regular and thorough entries of data. Each stock or entity should be entered as the only one listed on the file page. This author has two portfolios for stock data; a third is maintained for mutual funds and related investments. The following list of titles represents the current stock investment categories for research: Stock name and market symbol; address of corporate office; name of the designated official to contact; date and market price per share of stock; source of this data; date and percent of historical stock splits; date and percentage of future stock splits; name and address of market representative for source of weekly market data; products or services provided; public's acceptance of company; specific age of consumers; amount of stock in investor's portfolio; purchase cost per share and date purchased; name of brokerage and broker used; date discontinued in research program and reason.

On occasion, a stock may be discontinued in the research program due to weak performance, as related to the investor's goals referred to above. This author maintains 12 to 15 individual investments at all times to provide adequate researched data for the 20 to 25 active stocks invested. Data is collected daily when available and is posted in the research file every Saturday. After the investor becomes familiar with the program and the several investment entries being studied, the weekly postings shall require only a few minutes of time.

This author personally visits, on appointment, once prior to becoming an investor, each operating plant located within 100 miles, and every two years while owning stocks. Remember, as

5

an owner of stock, you are part owner of the company. Several company representatives have visited me at my home office during the tenure of stock ownership. Some have become highly treasured business friends.

PREPARE A RESEARCH PROGRAM
FOR INVESTING IN STOCKS

See article entitled "Research Procedures." Stocks have a history of returning greater growth over a considerable period of time than any other investment media. Therefore, an investor should make every effort to thoroughly understand stocks and the management of capital invested into stocks. Information may be obtained from your broker or direct from the company concerned in the study. The industry in which the company or entity operates; period of time the company has been operating; products or services offered by the company; performance of the stock over a period of several years; during a bear market; during a bull market; performance of the national economy during the above mentioned times.

A record system must be kept for each stock being considered. How has the stock performed in periods of stagnant economic conditions? In periods of strong economic conditions? The record should be set up to include each of the items mentioned in the above two paragraphs. A format should be selected that can be used for all stocks being considered in the research program. This author maintains three portfolios in his active file: Two are maintained for stock investments, and one for mutual funds and related investments. The same format should be used for all stocks being surveyed in order that continuity may exist.

The several items kept in the research file should be studied and reported into the record file once weekly. This author accumulates data as it becomes available during the week, and on Saturday he posts the entire data into the respective files for the stocks being researched.

On occasion a stock may be researched for several years before it is used as an investment. Or, a stock may be discarded from the research file because its performance is less than the standard prescribed by the investor.

Publications subscribed for include The Wall Street Journal and the Investors' Business Daily. Assistance may be had from investor friends who can share each issue as it arrives in the mail or from delivery boys. Several other monthly and quarterly publications are available to the investor. Cost of aides may be shared also.

Research Procedures

Research should always be processed prior to investing into a company or entity. The program is basically the same for both large and small companies or entities. We shall consider two aspects: For immediate investing and for investing several years in the future; all are considered to be for the individual investor.

A. Research procedures for immediate investing

This choice should be only a relatively small portion of your portfolio needs. The potential investment must be well established as a business program with a minimum of five previous consecutive years of qualified performance. Your references must be well established as an investigative medium for investors, both large and small. Your standards must be strong and include consistent annual earnings of up to your standards. The research program should include profits acquired annually; public's acceptance of products or programs produced; rate of growth; rank of company or entity in its industry and percentage of its market performance in comparison with that of competitors; status of executive personnel relative to their capabilities and comparison to the leadership of competitors within the industry. Each investor shall have his own particular

7

standards pertaining to excellence. This author has very high standards in all categories. It is an important reason why his success rate ranks especially high. He rates the research program prior to investing into a company or an entity as the most important part of the investment program.

B. Research procedures for several years prior to investing into a company or entity:

Each of the precepts outlined above for immediate investing shall also be performed for long term researching. Additionally, detailed records must be kept on file. The research program must be performed once weekly. This author keeps 12 or more companies or entities on file at all times. Some of the items researched may never be invested into. Others may be discarded because performance is below standards maintained. A separate record shall be maintained for each company or entity. (See C below.) Standardize the record keeping program so each company or entity has the same procedure.

C. This author maintains three portfolios with 8 to 10 companies or entities each, i.e., portfolio Number 3 consists of mutual funds and similar investments.

A useful and important resource for industry data regarding the above is Robert Morris Associates. This company publishes annual industry studies and annual statement studies in many industries. Write to them at One Liberty Place, 1650 Market Street, No. 2300, Philadelphia, PA 19103.

HOW TO CAPTURE INCORRUPTIBLE RESEARCH DATA

The Robert Morris Associates (RMA) Industry and Annual Statement Studies are independent national reports with which you can verify low, medium or high industry rank relative to annual assets and sales volume of various American industries.

It can be purchased for constant reference at the elbow of a dedicated investor. Write to Robert Morris Associates, One

Liberty Place, 1650 Market Street, Philadelphia, PA 19103. The volume has six levels of industry rank for various industries, not individual companies, in the United States. Your own research verification of any company's own statement of its rank as to comparative industry status, plus your broker's reports as to assets and sales volume annually over a minimum five-year period, and other independently published data regarding a company for your possible stock investment, in our opinion constitute incorruptible research data.

Using the SIMPL indicator categories, in a review of the company and its daily published stock market reports as to the company's stock price can further affect your decision to buy, not to buy, or to hold in abeyance for future action decisions.

The SIMPL indicators covered elsewhere in this book as being common to all investors' research efforts include: Sentiment, Interest Rates, Market momentum, Prices (consumer), and Low risk for the market. Of course, your own verification of a minimum five-year period of the company's industry rank, based on company statements including assets and sales volume during the period, as well as published stock values, either up or down; and indicators in published statements of growth factors for the company in addition to other market data, will reinforce your decisions.

MANAGING MUTUAL FUNDS TO BYPASS NEGATIVE MARKET

Many investors purchase mutual funds with the understanding that no management on the part of the investor shall ever take place. This plan of operation does not need to exist. For example, mutual fund holdings may be withdrawn from their regular position and moved into money market position without penalty or service charge by the mutual fund company. In the case of Fidelity Investments, there is a $5.00 service charge for each mutual fund for each transaction position in and out. Certainly it's minimal and should not be considered as a deterrent.

In September, 1995, this author considered the procedure at length and conferred with the sponsor, Fidelity Investments. For several weeks the general market continued to advance steadily. We reasoned that a correction should be expected at any time. The market took a slight reversal for two days and we moved all our mutual fund holdings from their regular positions into money market, all within the management of Fidelity. The entire assets were left in money market for 14 business days, so we moved the holdings out of money market to their former positions in mutual funds. After a week, the market again reversed its position and we again withdrew our holdings from their regular mutual fund positions and placed them into money market, where they remained as the market continued to decline for another 14 business days. After two positive market days, we again withdrew the entire money market assets and returned them to their original positions in mutual funds. Total service charge for the two movements for both of the two mutual funds: $20. The advantage to us as the investor was that for the total activity, we gained $300 per $10,000 invested during the week when the holdings were returned to their regular mutual fund position. The more important results that were realized during the experience was that while the assets were out of their regular mutual fund position and in money market position, a total of $1,500 per each $10,000 invested was by passed from being lost as a results of the declining market. Very simple, isn't it? Just know when to move!

YOUR FINANCIAL SUCCESS

Considerable of your financial success requires, for most, an entire adult lifetime. We cannot select a person who has become a financial success by how he, or he and his spouse, lives. The mode of living, or the kind of car, or home, or clothes, or the trips taken, do not denote one's success in investments. I have known numerous successful investors who had popular family members and contributed much to society during their respective lifetimes and following.

Certainly, a successful investor must have many of the traits of a winner. Early in life, this writer was taught many of the elements of being a winner. Foot racing was the medium of competition and experience. Many days were spent conditioning and training for each race. An attitude was acquired: To dislike a competitor; to dislike his achievements and how he obtained them. In the case of this winner, throughout his lifetime, an attitude of winning prevailed in most endeavors. Even today, after 12 years into retirement, there exists a preponderance of this competitive spirit. Hopefully, this phenomenon will continue. It is particularly impressive to understand that in the vast majority of people this experience does not even exist.

One's success in life does not altogether depend on ability and training; it also depends on determination to seize opportunities that occur and are available for the taking. It's one thing to read up on the principles of personal financial operations; but putting those principles to work is another matter. The issue is: Will you be a winner in the lifetime race for financial success? Or are you content to be a mere champion of wishful thinking? Many people go through life developing lists of good intentions. The winners are, in the meantime, busy putting their investment plans in motion, or in discarding that which is not applicable to make possible for their selections to be even more profitable. Experienced winners in the field of investments are prompt to acknowledge that for every successful investment player there are scores of those who have tried and failed. You have a choice: You can either take charge of all the money in your life -- and become a winner! -- or you can let opportunities slip through your fingers and get away.

A winner does not waste time fretting over financial

decisions. A winner approaches money decisions with confidence and studies all the options, considers the short and long term effects of different alternatives, then acts. A winner does not let irrelevant distractions interfere. Successful decision makers are ambitious, efficient, regularly check back on a previous decision to observe performance and productivity. The bottom line is to make decisions as to when to buy and when to sell. A winner must have the capability to do that which is prudent rather than that which may be the easy way.

The ability to create a financial empire is indeed rare. Only a few having the ability are willing to make personal sacrifices required to become a self-made millionaire. Certainly, one may be a lesser player and be well within the realm of a successful investor. Much depends on one's participation in community events on a regular basis.

It is important that each of us determine where we are in order that we can establish our realistic needs. We should not keep our accounts in four different banks, if one will suffice. However, that one choice must fully and effectively meet all needs.

We must always be alert to be on the lookout for hidden costs and excessive commissions. For example, why take out another insurance policy if we already have sufficient coverages in effect now?

INDICATOR CATEGORIES

Why use particular indicators? What is SIMPL Systems? We will consider SIMPL first. These form the SIMPL system:

Sentiment
Interest rates
Market momentum
Prices (consumer)
Low risk for market

All these five ingredients are common to all individual

investors. Mainly, it's a matter of having them in the proper perspective. To buy and sell investments is really very simple. Most investors end up making it entirely too complicated. I need not be technical. Most procedures having to do with trading are normal, well managed ways of life. We normally perform them individually on a daily basis. It's when we consider the impact and associate the process with money that many people clam up. So, market indicators must be studied by most and followed carefully. The emotions of fear and greed are probably most commonly responsible for most investment losses or failure to have profitable gains. Author never had financial earnings loss. There have been some low profit experiences when we had a sluggish market, but early liquidation prevented disaster. Fear sets in when rational thought becomes paralyzed and prevents the investor taking action at critical times. As timing is such an important part of success, the results can be disastrous. Conversely, favorable action involving critical timing often results in substantial profitable yields. A prime example of how fear entered into negative results was the 1982 bull market takeoff. Panic set in and many investors experienced very heavy losses. That market fell on people's fear. The world economies worsened the situation almost daily for some period of time. Greed played a prominent role.

Valid market indicators do much more than eliminate fear and greed. In assisting to accomplish that big task, they bring to bear a discipline that is highly useful for numerous other reasons. Knowing when and how much to invest in any market situation is equally as important in periods when fear or greed aren't rampant as when they are.

The 1983-84 interim stock market period top rank, in hindsight, was one that could be ignored. Many of my astute investment friends, as well as this investor, ignored the period and sat out the dilemma. Our results were merely a slowed growth, but no losses. Of course, we made no liquidations during that time. The market correction period lasted less than 8 months. That kind of market points up the importance of investors making strong use of positive market conditions. An excellent period of positive performance was during 1991. That was my lifetime best, mainly because I could spend much time in studying the situation. My broker enjoyed having me telephone him. His commissions on my trading alone were over $1,780. We bought and sold many times that year.

Another major value of using valid indicators is their ability to control informed opinion about market trends. These are the opinions that most seasoned investors do continually employ. Floods of available data certainly confuse the proper picture. That points up the fact that sorting out the facts is probably the greatest task of all. Vast amounts of irrelevant material must be discarded or certainly not considered. So, informed opinion can get an investor in trouble if the improper information is used as a guiding influence.

The most successful market professionals have established some form of filtering discipline that advises them which piece of the data bank is useful and which should be ignored. An hour spent per week properly selecting the prime procedure should be sufficient. Only rarely, when the indicators are on alert, should it require as much as two or three hours per week. As a result, I allot but one hour per week for this detail.

The final reason for using market indicators is that only through them a multi-market, asset allocation concept can function. The asset allocation decisions should be carefully planned. Your investment goal should consider the maximum amount of risk which shall be allowed for each different element of investments.

This author closely tracks the broad small-cap market in behalf of his growth and with positions of merit in industries.

The tide turns for Value Funds. Yesterday's darlings have slumped this year. Investors get suckered into performance. The odds are that the top performing holdings in one cycle won't be on top in the next go-around. Today's winners are value funds, whose portfolios tend to be full of companies with below average price/book and price/earnings ratios. Such funds have not been stung as severely in the market correction, having been off only about 1% on average this year. Value funds seem a logical choice in this environment. Historically, we got a higher return with but slightly lower risk, so it's like getting something for nothing! Best seller author, Bill Donoghue, believes current portfolio performance trends indicate value funds have value. Value fund managers tend to be individual stock pickers, and they will have more success now than those who screen for companies with accelerating earnings. Someone who is selective can find opportunities, and with rising interest rates, it will be difficult for growth funds to succeed. Another fund manager builds his portfolio to reduce interest rate and market risk. A suggestion for value funds is that they are better suited for tax-deferred retirement accounts than taxable accounts, due to their higher rates of current taxable income, compared with capital gains-oriented growth funds.

Positive economic fundamentals in global growth and inflation outweigh the geopolitical wildcards. For investors seeking a mainstream international fund, Warburg, Pincus International Equity has performed well in past down markets, and returned 32% to shareholders for the 12 months ending June 30, 1994.

The real role of bonds in a diversified portfolio for a long-term use is to offset the risk of stocks. Short-term bonds offer 90% of the return of intermediate bonds with much less risk. Doing nothing is the most costly strategy of any.

INTEREST RATE SWINGS

Interest rates rise and bond yields fall. It's a scenario that may be all too familiar to you. Now for a simple example.

Suppose you buy a new $1,000 bond. It pays $80 interest a year, so your yield is normally 8%. Now, assume that market interest rates rise 2% to 10%. There is only one way for your bond to adjust to that rate. Its market price must fall to $800. At that price, your $80 annual interest produces a new market yield of 10%. Conversely, if market interest rates fall back to 8%, your bond's price will rise again to $1,000. Result: Interest rates up, bond prices (bond fund prices) down. Rates down, prices up. Simple.

If you own more than one fund, you're aware that some fall faster than others when interest rates rise. Then how can you determine how exposed your bond funds are to interest rate swings? Analysts use several methods to compute a complex system. "Duration" measures the present value of the future income flows on a bond fund's investments. Benham's duration is 16 years, which aims is half that, about 8 years. The lesson: Minimize durations to minimize price changes. Most bond funds will advise you of their duration upon request. Give them a call.

BEATING BONDS

"Blessed are the young for they shall inherit the national debt," by President Herbert Hoover. The problem is the same as during Hoover's era only now the problem with the debt is that it now is huge. The federal government spends about 25% of its annual budget on debt servicing; U. S. Corporations spend nearly 22% of their cash flow on debt service. The former is an all-time high and the latter is at a level seen only at the bottom of a depression. The pair represent a staggering burden to bear considering the annual interest payments, much worse when considering pay-off of the debts. When we won't be able to borrow the amount of the interest, we'll be broke. We're getting close, but perhaps surprisingly, U. S. Government debt quality is still arguably among the best in the world. The presumption remains that its interest and principle will be paid. Never mind that it may be paid with drastically depreciated dollars and/or new taxes. Most everyone presumes it will be paid.

A bond represents debt. The single aspect of U. S. government bonds, then, that bond buyers worry least about, is their credit risk. This may become a wrongly ignored trepidation, but for now, the assumption we must make is that the U. S. Government is good for the bucks.

To be certain, credit risk, or rating, is important for any bond issuer, and must be addressed in considering most bonds. Market professionals use bond rating services to quantify this element, and that's where the AAA to D bond ratings, or variations on those letters, come into play. For our purposes, though, we want to eliminate as many factors in our bond investment decisions as possible. We'll focus for the moment on U. S. Treasuries for that reason and for their ready marketability.

Bonds are one leg of our three-market concept for the simple reason that they represent a pure play on the deflation (or disinflation) economic scenario. In this aspect, bonds cover the reverse side of the inflation coin. They perform best in price when inflation rates are perceived to be declining. As noted earlier, the history of the past 10 years shows this has been a rare event. But, longer stretches of modern history, large parts of the 20s and 30s, for example, found bonds performing very well. And the anti-inflation stance in Washington, D.C., since 1989 has made them important market winners during a large part of the 1990s. The second part of bond risk is inflation.

CURRENT RECESSION

The impact of the current recession certainly is severe. Nothing is good about a recession; but it isn't all bad! As a result of all the difficulties and delays, it makes us do a better job of managing, of budgeting, of meeting our obligations as human beings.

I fully realize that this immediate area is relatively in good circumstances; that the recession is comparably light here. But, our economy has slowed considerably. Real Estate activity has slowed, employment is lower than usual for this season, people are traveling less than usual. However, signs of the times are improving. Business activity is improving; people's attitudes and opinions are gradually improving. The old adage, "Everything is Gonna Turn Out OK," is still basic.

MONEY MANAGEMENT CHOICES

Money Management Choices offer many ways to save money and accumulate earnings over a period of time. Using a mutual fund and a regular deposit fits many who are still working. This method is commonly called Dollar-Cost-Averaging. Many advantages result from this plan. One can invest as he earns. One may begin by investing a lump sum. We will assume that the investor puts the same amount of capital to work monthly; say $100 each month. One can arrange with his bank to monthly send $100 to the mutual fund company to be credited to your account, or one may choose to send a check for $100 monthly. The important thing is that the same amount is invested monthly. When the program becomes established, it means that more shares will be purchased at a low cost and fewer shares at a high cost. This will provide a true average cost of investing over a period of time. If the market eventually improves, and it always has, there will be growth by capital gains which will not be determined until the time of liquidation. This system doesn't require brilliance or luck, only discipline to invest monthly, *on the same day, monthly*.

One may also Dollar-Cost-Average with larger lump-sum investments. If you have $50,000 to invest and would be more comfortable to take more time to deposit the sum, it is very simple to send but $10,000 monthly for five months, or even longer. Almost any plan can be arranged. It is simple to use the telephone, toll free number.

It is common procedure for a mutual fund to carry the shares purchased out to the third decimal point, which allows you to really invest on a Dollar-Cost-Average. If such a plan is put into practice early in one's working days, he will likely find that he and his spouse will become financially independent many years earlier than anticipated.

RESEARCHING STOCKS FOR FUTURE INVESTMENT

Research of previous performance of stocks is of prime importance to the investor whose goal is' to have creditable earnings over the long term. Some goals must necessarily be made. This author has developed high standards over the years which is largely responsible for his success as an investor, teacher and author in the broad segment of the investment industry.

A prime ingredient for strong yields is the selection of successful companies or entities. We shall consider only business activity within the United States in our discussion. An interesting observation: the comparison of stocks, corporate bonds, and government bonds in comparison to inflation which determines the purchasing power of earnings. This author for the past 20 years has established a goal of 20% growth annually. He has successfully achieved that goal every year except 1994 when his earnings were 19.8%. In 1994, less than 3% of individual American investors had a profitable year. 1996 proved to be his lifetime highest annual return.

Historically, investing in the stock of U. S. companies has not only out-paced inflation but offered the long-term investor greater overall returns than other types of investments.

THE ADVANTAGES OF STOCK MUTUAL FUNDS

Stock mutual funds offer the advantages of professional managemnet, diversification, and liquidity. A mutual fund's management team has access to proprietary research that can enhance its expertise in identifying market opportunities. Diversified portfolios can reduce the risk of owning just a few stocks while offering the potential for significant long-term results. Finally, shares of mutual funds are easily redeemed for cash. Of course, past performance is no guarantee of future results, and you may have a gain or loss when you sell your shares.

PLAN AHEAD FOR TAX LIABILITY

We always prepare our Record Book by early December for a preliminary review with our accountant. We project several possible transactions as to how they will affect our Investment Income for the year, should they be consummated during the final month of the year. For instance, early last December, we met with our accountant (on December 3rd), for such review. The activity for the 11 months just past had income level from investments to put us into a tax bracket somewhat higher than we had anticipated. Furthermore, additional investment income during December would aggravate the situation still more. So, a review of our portfolio revealed that one company's stock (100 shares) was purchased somewhat earlier than others and at a substantially higher per share cost. So we liquidated the 100 shares at the depressed market price for a net loss which reflected our earnings for the entire year at the level of the lower tax rate. Needless to say, we had no additional liquidations during December, as it really was a depressed stock market.

In addition to the normal transaction details involved in this above described sale of common stock, an important additional request was made by us to the broker. We described our situation as to why we desired to take a capital loss in the liquidation and then requested from him a description of the stock sold as to amount, when purchased, purchase cost, sale date, liquidation price per share, etc. (Brokers are familiar with this provision in the Internal Revenue Code relative to investors in stocks and bonds. The informational data the broker provided in this instance is "Specific Identification." This kind of transaction is outlined in an article, "A Primer for Fund Investors at Tax Time," by Tom Herman, and published in Western Edition of The Wall Street Journal for Friday, March 15, 1991, distributed from the Journal's Federal Way, WA, publishing branch.

Many other valuable references of IRS Code for Investors are referenced in this article. I suggest you retain it in your investment file for future reference. Always remember, however, to check with your accountant or the IRS as to whether the Code still has the same rule before you or your accountant prepares the tax return. The IRS can revise the rules at any time without notice.

I telephoned my friend at the IRS office locally about another important consideration about the Wall Street Journal article. The article covers, principally, investors' activities in mutual funds. My interpretation is that the author referenced mutual funds consistently in the article for the reason that, tax-wise, mutual funds are more complex and more in depth than are stocks and bonds. Anyhow, the same rules apply to both.

Remember, you must complete the qualification details (described above) during the year the liquidation transaction is processed in order to fully qualify for the benefits offered. Later is too late.

RETIRING IN FINANCIAL DIGNITY

Additional Income Needed (in Dollars) at Retirement with Various Inflation Rates:

Years Until Retirement	5%	8%	10%	12%	15%
10	1.63	2.16	2.59	3.11	4.05
11	1.71	2.33	2.85	3.48	4.65
12	1.80	2.52	3.14	3.90	5.35
13	1.89	2.72	3.45	4.36	6.15
14	1.98	2.94	3.80	4.89	7.08

Years Until Retirement	5%	8%	10%	12%	15%
15	2.08	3.17	4.18	5.47	8.14
16	2.18	3.43	4.60	6.13	9.36
17	2.29	3.70	5.05	6.87	10.77
18	2.41	4.00	5.56	7.69	12.38
19	2.53	4.32	6.12	8.61	14.23
20	2.65	4.66	6.73	9.65	16.37
21	2.79	5.03	7.4	10.80	18.82
22	2.93	5.44	8.14	12.10	21.64
23	3.07	5.87	8.95	13.55	24.89
24	3.23	6.34	9.85	15.18	28.63
25	3.39	6.85	10.83	17.00	32.92
26	3.56	7.4	11.92	19.04	37.86
27	3.73	7.99	13.11	21.32	43.54
28	3.92	8.63	14.42	23.88	50.07
29	4.12	9.32	15.86	26.75	57.58
30	4.32	10.06	17.45	29.96	66.22
31	4.54	10.87	19.19	33.56	76.14
32	4.76	11.74	21.11	37.58	87.57
33	5.00	12.68	23.23	42.09	100.70
34	5.25	13.69	25.55	47.14	115.80
35	5.52	14.79	28.10	52.80	133.18

U. S. Department of Interior

One dollar spent for goods today will require the above dollars to purchase the same goods years ahead. Will you be ready?

FORMULA FOR FINANCIAL INDEPENDENCE

Consider that inflation is the American Free Enterprise way. Then Time + Money + American Free Enterprise = Opportunity to Become Financially Independent. I have used this formula for many years and it has proven to be very valuable. It is regularly used by estate planners and investment planners among others. But one must be honest and realistic concerning all the facts and estimates.

Time - Ingredient Number One. If you are young and only have a small amount of capital to invest, don't despair. Accept

22

that which cannot be changed. You possess one of the most important ingredients for financial independence -- TIME. Savings of but $30 per month started at age 25 can equal $90 per month started at age 35, $300 at age 45; and $1,275 per month started at age 55. If we calculate the importance of time in reverse, savings of $50 per month for 10 years at 12% will add up to a sum that is less than savings of $25 a month for 15 years.

Perhaps you already have $10,000 saved. Let's look at the difference time makes in the amount of capital you will accumulate (exclusive of taxes).

INVESTMENT GOALS

YEARS	AT 12%
10	$ 31,058
20	96,462
30	299,599
40	930,509

U. S. Department of Commerce

These figures emphasize the importance of starting as early as you can to reach your predetermined goal of financial independence. I hope that you learned at an early age the importance of putting each day to maximum use.

Money -- Ingredient Number Two. The second ingredient of my formula for financial independence is MONEY. You have it every payday, or you may have acquired it through previous efforts of your own or from your industrious and generous ancestors. Your next challenge is to put this money to work for yourself as hard as you had to work to get it. To become financially independent, you must save regularly and make your money grow. Unfortunately, I observe many people who save and let institutions grow, building magnificent skyscrapers that add impressively to our skylines.

American Free Enterprise -- Ingredient Number Three. This brings us to the third ingredient of my formula for financial independence. By investing your money in American free enterprise, you can benefit directly from the enormous productivity, growth, and wealth of our GREAT ECONOMY. The ultimate purpose of this book is to provide you with the knowledge and the tools to do just that: To teach you how you can own your share of American industry, energy, communications systems technology, agriculture, and a wide variety of other viable investments.

You have seen how important time is in accomplishing your investment goal. Now let us introduce another important factor, the rate of return. The rate of return that you receive on your funds will be determined by how skillfully you, or the professional adviser who helps you, are in putting your money to work. Let's look at the difference an additional 5% per year return can make in your results:

$100 per Month Invested at 10% and 15%

Years	At 10%	At 15%	Difference
10	$ 21,037	$ 28,018	$ 6,981
20	75,602	141,372	65,770
30	217,131	599,948	382,817
40	584,222	2,455,144	1,870,922

What an amazing difference 5% makes!! One of the best ways to obtain a graphic picture of the importance of the rate of return is to study compound interest tables. Compound interest tables are fascinating. Compound interest may be the eighth wonder of the world! We will cover compound interest later.

MANAGING STOCKS

An automobile can be one's best friend or, carelessly used or managed, can be a vicious killer and a very costly machine. So it is with common stocks. Stocks can be one's best friend and an important avenue toward financial security and financial independence.

24

COMPONENT PARTS OF WEALTH

Some specific facts are basic: it is reasonable to have a goal, or rather a minimum goal of earning at least 20% annually. It would require slightly less than five years to double the assets provided you obtain at least 20% return annually. Certainly this is realistic. I have many friends who have been doing that for many years. So, everyone can expect to become richer. You must have one important feature: discipline to save. Also you must want to study and enjoy a life span of sufficient length of time. Many of the things you do will be pleasant and will be repeated over and over again. Mostly one must be satisfied with the kinds of things that are not costly, or cost but little or nothing. One must learn to be satisfied with that which is around him: to travel but slightly. After all, modern living brings global scenes into the home daily. A favorite television program of mine is portrayed in Honolulu, Hawaii, by a person who speaks excellent English. All who are interviewed also speak fine English.

Component Parts in Dollars. One million is 1,000 multiplied by 1,000. During the early years of saving, accumulation of capital is slow. Through determination, stamina and repetition, one will be able to feel remarkable progress by middle age.

During these proceedings, we shall consider that *no investment funds shall be borrowed*. First, today's cost for borrowing is entirely excessive to the investor. So, we will endeavor to select investments which return 20% or more annually and have a relatively low risk. This combination is out there. It is a matter of locating them. Remember, business must have capital constantly and is in agreement that interest must be paid for the use of capital. So there are several important features already set into motion. We shall determine that yield shall include both dividends and increase or Growth in market value. Use of investment income as compounding Growth shall always be put to full use. It really is great that one of the common tools

25

of mathematics is "compound interest." Also, it is often a great tool to be able to leave proceeds from Growth capital in as part of an investment until the liquidation of the investment. If an investment is liquidated on January 2nd, Income Taxes thereon aren't payable to Internal Revenue Service until April of the following year. I have used this tool many times. The opportunity is there; it's only a matter of using it. Remember Benjamin Franklin's words: "Money is of a prolific generating nature - money can beget money, and its offspring can beget more." For the purpose of our calculations, for any taxes that must be paid on investment earnings, it would be economical to use capital from another source with which taxes may be paid.

SHARPEN YOUR TALENTS; TIME IS ON YOUR SIDE; MOVE AHEAD NOW

We are all privileged to have many talents. Perhaps it would be appropriate to evaluate some of the qualities successful people have. The art of deducing is to reason from the general to the particular. To become skillful in our powers of deduction requires practice over time. There shall always remain the challenge to improve. This precept shall ever remain our driving force. Nature provides that our judgments may be fallible, liable to error. Severity of error and repetition by individuals are the variables. It remains for us to prepare ourselves, make important decisions and progress in our goals. If one attains a goal quickly, or with extreme ease, then perhaps the objectives were inadequate.

Time passed by shall never recur; the mold is already set. That which remains is our time. One's remaining time is his to improve. Only the latter is for us to influence. That which is behind us shall serve as patterns to guide us. That's what education is all about. We are indeed fortunate that our predecessors strove for progress and left valuable records of their achievements. It remains for one to select the proper route to

26

follow. Once your route is selected, it remains forever a challenge to become knowledgeable and a master of timing. That is a brief definition of success in investing. When a facet of this formula is perfected, it only remains for one to repeat, repeat, and repeat.

Incorruptible information which is applicable for use in your performance should make a record in your notes. Therefore, it is highly important to develop a file or notebook into which such memoranda may be entered and referenced properly for future use. The index becomes a vital ingredient to the text.

Over the years there has been a broad assortment of incentives which prompted people to save and invest. More recently, and certainly now, and undoubtedly for years to come, the impact of Income Tax and Inflation make investing almost essential to enable one to live with dignity during the retirement years. We are indeed fortunate to have many important influences developing to make for an improved outlook in the World Economy as never before. The impact of a United State of Europe is rapidly coming into existence. That will greatly influence and expand World Trade, including that of the United States. Transportation and technology have improved remarkably around the globe. Living standards of most peoples have improved to higher standards than ever before. The 1991 recession has been relatively mild and of short duration in the United States as well as around the World. These and other factors give promise for the next 20 years to be the best ever for business, trade, human relations, and for investments and investors. Growth shall come more rapidly, and into more avenues of commerce than ever before.

How fast can we expect our savings to grow? To double in volume? Of course, there is no uniform pace or standard of time. So, the challenge to progress is maintained by the investor. His selection of investments from the myriad of assorted possibilities; the yield and his success will be determined by all

27

of these factors. Some simple, basic facts are well established: It takes only an average return of 10% compounded to double your assets in 7.2 years. At 12% it takes six years; at 18%, four years; and at 24%, three years. Remember, the process includes compounded interest. Tax liability is to be paid from other sources. Most prudent investors set their goals in excess of 20%. So, there are many avenues of investment selections, modes of investment earnings, growth, risk, tax considerations; market prices, trends, fluctuations and economic influences. To many investors, the complexity of important factors, amount of time required, lack of self confidence to make important decisions, inability to perform proper research, are all valid reasons why individual investors engage others to work for them.

SUCCESS INSTINCT PUT TO USE

It may be inane or inordinate or just plain hard work and meticulous supervision to be successful in managing your own investments. It is my firm belief that it is unequivocally the latter, particularly when evaluated over a long period of time. That is the way my success came to be. That is the way my colleagues acquired their wealth, in the main.

Successful people have a built-in guidance system, or goal-striving device. I prefer the thought of having a precise, well planned goal. Basically, a strong faith involves belief in our great nation and forever having an optimistic outlook.

Man's creative imagination is unique to man. Animals don't have it. Perhaps at some time in our lives, we can apply creative imagination and experience and wealth of education to come up with success. Certainly, some of the success in investing comes from much of the latter.

It always helps if an individual has a positive viewpoint and a positive outlook. To plan ahead it is always a great start if one thinks positively. Add common sense and good judgment to time and the result will usually be favorable. For the overall pattern of life must include happiness. That which causes one to be happy may not necessarily be that which causes another to be happy. Or for one, the ingredients of happiness may be the combined effects of several motives or objectives. So, we are all quite different. And so our objectives may be quite different. An important part of life is to not place severe limits on accomplishments. Let us not be too proud to accept help from others. Two heads may be better than one. We should not be so calloused as not to offer help to others. They probably will appreciate the assistance.

Emptiness of life is a symptom that you are not living creatively. You either have no goal that is important enough to you, or you are not using your talents and efforts in striving toward an important goal. It is the person who has no purpose of his own who pessimistically concludes, "Life has no purpose." It is the person who has no goal worth working for who concludes, "life is not worthwhile." It is the person with no important job to do who complains, "There is nothing to do." The individual who is actively engaged in a struggle, or in striving toward an important goal, does not come up with pessimistic philosophies concerning the meaninglessness or the futility of life. So, select a worthwhile goal and go after it!

Choose and maintain a profitable portfolio through diversification. The word means spreading your risks. The old adage of not putting all your eggs in one basket has much merit in assembling a good, profitable portfolio. Don't put all your faith in one company, or in one industry. You don't want to be disappointed or dismayed. If you buy a diversified group of fundamentally sound stocks with good earnings and growth, the chances are that in an average or better market conditions that one can catch at least some of the big winners, since most big gains in a diversified portfolio comes from one or two big winners You should strive for a portfolio covering a wide range of industries, with only one or two at the most, within a single industry within a country.

When managing your own portfolio, you will find it extremely helpful to limit your portfolio to 10 stocks, regardless of the amount of capital invested. For a sizeable account, it is convenient to own more than 1,000 shares of a single company. Remember that the reason we think in terms of 100 shares, commonly called a round lot, is because there usually is a price advantage for 100 or more shares purchased at once. Over diversification may lead to being unable to keep up often enough with developments with all companies. I like to always have two or three companies in abeyance and ready to bring into the portfolio when needed; a simple way to upgrade a portfolio is to liquidate the low earners and retain the leaders. By so doing, you gradually move to a position of strength. Nothing can be more gratifying than to have a portfolio with all holding in a position of strong earnings.

INVESTORS CAN MANAGE THEIR MUTUAL FUNDS

Individual investors can manage their mutual fund holdings provided they know and understand and also have the skills of properly timing difficult procedures. During the second half of 1994, a vast majority of mutual funds declined along with the market trend and ended the year with negative results. This author was aware as early as mid-May that the second half of the year would be an unusually dull market and that mutual funds would likely suffer in the projected decline. That outlook was confirmed by a dozen or more of his broker and money market manager acquaintances located around the nation. By May 16, he had cleared with Fidelity Investments, the mutual fund company, for a service fee of $5.00 per fund, an investor owner could exchange his holdings with other Fidelity-managed entities. A single money market fund with a projected 5% annual earnings was selected to receive all capital from the three growth mutual funds. The capital then positioned in the money market holding remained until late November when the general market showed signs of having completed its correction and advanced regularly. Also, this investor chose to resume the holdings in their initial position -- the three same growth mutual funds. Results? Considerable losses were bypassed. Gain for the entire year for the three mutual funds was on an average of 13.83% for 1994. The portion of his portfolio invested in common stocks also responded quite well, including 500 shares of Microsoft Corporation which split 2 for 1. His total portfolio yielded 17.9% for 1994. Each above mentioned professional friend telephones to inquire of the year's results. In summary, that performance and results were probably a lifetime high. There have been many stronger gains, but none with such results.

Personal Portfolios

The author maintains three separate portfolios arranged as to amount of time necessary and ease of management. For example, mutual funds records are filed in Number 3 as only a slight amount of time and effort is required to manage the account. Each portfolio has 12 to 15 different companies' records. A filing cabinet of four shelves is maintained for portfolio materials only. Also, a file for previous years is maintained there with Federal Income Tax data. A separate file cabinet is maintained for all other records and research data.

Simple and easy-to-locate records and other vital data are maintained at all times. The appropriate records are used each business day together with other reports obtained by TV or in the mail. Many contacts are made easily via toll-free long distance telephone. To clarify a message, the author's wife is always simultaneously on another telephone. Follow-up confirmation of each transaction by mailed record is carefully audited with notes written at the time the telephone transaction is consummated. Prompt filing of all business data is regularly performed. All business mailings are kept current and in details adequate for the need.

On date of December 15, 1995, we purchased a computer manufactured by Compaq Company and distributed at South Center Shopping Mall, near Seattle. Model is Compaq Presario Number 7170. Accessories include VCR for TV, printer, keyboard and miscellaneous others. Total cost of $3,227.72. Our friend and computer specialist, Ted Frees, attended us in purchase of the set and assembled it in our home and taught us several lessons on its use prior to teaching us in a course at Southeast Seattle Senior Center in seven lessons. We liquidated 100 shares of Microsoft at $391.00 per share. Shares had split 2 for 1 with purchase cost of $29.08 per share. The new computer will be used in recording this book, "The New Investor's Bible," beginning in early January 1997.

1995 was an excellent year for investors. Our holdings yielded over 32.6%. It was a very good year to transfer some of our holdings from a regular account to Investors Retirement Reserves Account, as it was required that the regular account holdings be liquidated prior to repurchasing into the new account. We are again well diversified with our entire three portfolios.

The New Investors' Bible represents the "Master Book" among 20 books written by the author from 1991 to 1996, all on the subject of investments. During that six-year period, the investment market experienced in 1991 its outstanding year during the lifetime of the author for strong investment gains. He experienced maximum returns of his 55 years of investing of his personal portfolios. The fiscal year ending September 30, 1991, proved to be his most profitable lifetime high. Assets of his three personal portfolios were turned over three times during the 10-month period. Professional investors and money market advisers from around the nation were in agreement that 1991 would likely be a strong and profitable year for investors. The author's earnings for the fiscal year October 1, 1990, to September 30, 1991, were 161.7%

During October 1990, he liquidated most of his slowest gaining investment holdings and placed them into money market. The low valued stocks which were researched previously began to show life and started to gain in value. The favored large companies of Western Washington State were purchased and held for a period of about three months. As their rate of growth slowed, liquidations were made and replacement stocks included those of medium sized companies. As their earnings increased and continued for three to four months and gradually slowed, they were liquidated and replaced with stocks of small aggressive companies. As the rate of growth slowed among those smaller companies, they were liquidated and replaced with holding which were planned for long-term ownership. And so the fiscal year ended with the results as stated above. All investments employed during the banner year experience were stocks of the Puget Sound region for the reason that the area had declined least of all other areas of the United States during the recession period immediately preceding the beginning of the fiscal period referred to above. Status of economic conditions over a time are very important in planning for investment growth.

Quite different were the economic conditions during 1994 when the investment market reversed into a prolonged decline for several months. Less than 3% of individual investors experienced a profitable year in 1994. Again, the author retained Pacific Northwest companies' stocks in his portfolios for the entire calendar year. He had a growth of 18.9% for 1994. It was the lowest amount of growth he experienced in more than two decades. However, he believes the year resulted in his outstanding performances, considering all the serious obstacles that existed during the period.

Many other significant features which took place during the six years, 1991 through 1996, are treated in the book. The book has been prepared as an advanced reference for new and experienced individual investors. It is intended to serve as a ready reference and should be retained in your personal library for you and for posterity.

Your Role as an Investor

Self Discipline must be practiced at all times if you expect to be a winner in the field on money management. The secret of financial independence isn't brilliance, but the discipline to save a part or all you earn and to put it to work in shares of American industry, real estate, and others. Self-discipline helps you to achieve goals. It also is a mental and physical process. It's your own visualization of your predetermined worthwhile goal of financial independence. The successful people I know seem to find their accomplishments not too difficult and often surprisingly easy, simply because it seems so few are really trying. Winners look at life as a game they expect to win, desire to win, are prepared to win and know how to win. They have nurtured and developed the habit of winning. They make a concerted effort every day that they are self-determined. They have an intense desire to do everything that contributes toward success; and to do it very well.

1. Over-caution is the enemy of success. Over-caution should be avoided whenever possible in the plan to be a winner. The person who takes no chances must usually take that which is left after the others have finished choosing. Not to win is not a sin, but not to try is a tragedy. It is well established that companies that are the most successful have a bias toward action; they are willing to take risks because they realize there is no reward without risk. If you have never missed when investing, you haven't been trying strong enough; or you have been holding weak entities much too long for maximum profits. Play the money game well, but never ultra-conservatively. Many people are not successful investors because they are afraid to do anything at all with their capital; so they just leave it in a fixed guaranteed position for years, where the ravages of inflation and taxation destroy it. That certainly is not playing it safe -- that's simply playing it dumb!

2. Knowledge is crucial to success. Think as you build your financial plan around your goals. Don't guess. Information in our communication society is available on almost any subject that you need to be informed about. So put as much accurate information together as possible, and then act on it. Every financial plan is different; but, in general, there are two rules that always apply: 1. Build your capital and add to your nest egg while you are young. Remember to pay yourself first; and don't spend the nest egg. While you are young, a few dollars invested will yield as much as many dollars will when you are age 50 or more. Never consider any of your earnings on investments as spendable until you have reached your goal of financial independence. This is how to develop your money power. Money is a medium of exchange and it is the harvest of your production.

3. Ignorance about money. Another reason for failing is ignorance of what money must do to accomplish a financial goal. We are raising a generation of financial illiterates. Even many

college graduates cannot figure simple percentages. They simply do not know how to manage money. It's sad, but very true. They must learn this fundamental to successful living in our system of free enterprise.

4. Failure to learn our tax laws. Failure to learn and apply our tax laws is a common deficiency of Americans. Money you get to spend, whether for groceries or for investments, is money you have earned and which our government allows you to keep after taxes. So, learn the rules of the money and tax game.

5. Life Insurance--the wrong kind. People fail to become financially independent because they buy entirely too much, or the wrong kind, of life insurance. Many people are insurance poor. Perhaps they cannot pay all of the premium and have to drop the policy. That can be very costly. Get smart on life insurance. Don't buy until you know.

6. Failure to develop a winning mentality. People also fail to win the money game because they fail to develop a winning mentality. The demarcation line between success and failure is often very narrow. It can be crossed if the desire to succeed can be stimulated, if competent guidance is available, and if sufficient encouragement and incentive are provided. There are many vital parts to the psychology of winning, but some of the most important for financial independence are attitude, effort, lack of prejudice, persistence, enthusiasm, the ability to make a decision, and self-discipline. Very often followers fail to have confidence and cannot make decisions on their own. They wait for others to analyze the situation and make a serious decision. One's place among his siblings has a substantial influence. For instance, this author was the eldest child among three younger sisters. Also, boys are often more aggressive than are girls. So, many influences often exist in very early life.

Attitude is truly a magic word that you should place not only in your vocabulary but also in the very fiber of your being if you desire to be successful in the realm of money or in any other important area of your life. You will shape your own financial life by the attitudes that you hold each day. If one has a poor attitude about studying money management, you won't learn very much until you change that attitude. If an attitude of failure predominates, you are defeated before you start. Look around and study successful people. They will go sailing through life from one success to another. Successful people have an attitude that they can accomplish whatever they set out to do. And because of this attitude, they do accomplish their goals and achieve some very remarkable gains in life.

Effort on your part is vital, because to become a good investor you must seriously apply your intelligence, use your ability to acquire knowledge, and give your attention to details and timing. If you cannot, will not, or do not have the ability to do these things successfully for yourself, don't take a distorted ego trip by not admitting that someone else can do something better than you can do it. Select a capable, competent and reliable professional to work for you. Investing, properly approached with constant supervision, is in my opinion the safest long-term option for money. Speculation, on the other hand, can be risky., Cost of investment advice and services can be funds very well spent when really needed.

Lack of prejudice also is an important attribute of the psychology of winning. We all have prejudices, but we should continuously work to rid ourselves of them. In studying details of an investment, some say, "If only I didn't have to bother with the facts!" The fact is that the explanatory details are probably the most important part of the entirety.

Persistence and follow-through. Most winners possess these attributes as part of a winning solution. If you begin a financial planning program and experience a temporary setback, of all things, don't give up to take a neutral position; stick with it; give the program an opportunity to demonstrate its worth.

Remember time is an important ingredient of successful investing.

Ability to make a decision. This is an important characteristic of successful investing. Competent leaders usually are quick to make a decision after having all the facts, but are slow to change that decision later. Yesterday is past. The record is fact.

Anticipating Market Trends

Since the stock market cycles around an intrinsic value, after it has fallen in a given year, there is only a slight probability of it falling further during the next year. In fact, pressure is actually created by a down year that drives the market upward in the following years. The market discounts bad news, such as war, recession, inflation, into share prices. When the bad news becomes reality, there is nowhere to go but up. So, people who buy stocks at such time make a killing over 90% of the time. This principle can be applied to the long-term investor to greatly increase returns. Given the consistency of market recoveries, an aggressive investor might want to periodically leverage his portfolio to take advantage of the cycles. In this instance, the investor may need to borrow part of his needs, but he should purchase heavily after the prices of stocks have seriously declined. He will then be in position with his entire portfolio to enjoy the price rise for the next several months. The logical periods for leverage would be those two-year periods that follow down years in the DJIA, as market returns are obviously superior in those years. Over time, returns have been 36% to 38% for each of the two years following the years of slump. In conclusion, leverage can substantially enhance the aggressive investor's earnings during two years which follow a year or more of price slump.

There are many timing tools which can be used as techniques in managing your investments. All of them require that you follow the market prices diligently every market business day. A thorough keeping of records is always a must. Success usually follows a disciplined effort applied consistently over time.

THE RETIREMENT YEARS

We have obtained a visual picture of what the potentials are with compounding over a period of years, and maintaining 20% interest rate over the entire term.

Successful people do things that they don't like to do in order to accomplish the things they want to accomplish in the fields of investments. Successful people are motivated by pleasing results. Failures search for pleasing experiences and are satisfied with the results that they can obtain by doing the things they like to do. We must assume that your purpose is to become wealthier. That your purpose is strong enough to make you form the habit of doing certain thing you don't like to do in order to attain this goal.

To have maximum creativity your body must have pure air, wholesome food, adequate exercise, and creative thoughts. The successful investor does many things to further the success of his investment program. Remember, he is motivated by successful achievements. It takes a lot of study to become knowledgeable. You can do it, too. If it makes you financially independent, that will be a major accomplishment of which you can be justly proud.

PLANNING FOR YOUR RETIREMENT

Your financial life can be divided into three periods: your "Learning Period", your "Yearning Period" and your retirement or "Golden" Period." Whether the third period of your life will be "golden" or "yearning" will, in all probability, be determined by the financial decisions you make during your earning period.

Aging is becoming more of a burden. We are living much

39

longer than at any previous time. Presently, the actual income of 3.3 million seniors over age 65 is under the poverty level ($4,979 for a single person over age 65, including Social Security). The median income for males over 65, including Social Security, is $10,450, and the figure for females is $4,020. Cost of living is rising. Being broke is a devastating experience -- especially when youth has escaped.

The likelihood of your living to an older age is increasing. In 1990, 12.7% of the population will be in the poverty group. There were 31.5 million elderly in 1990. The number will double early next century. There are more over age 75 years. Better medical care, better nutrition, more attention to fitness and exercise, a more positive mental attitude about maturity and retirement, and several other factors contribute. It is up to each of us to add more life to our years.

SPECIFIC STRATEGY

A specific strategy must be planned for all of us who yearn to be wealthy and live a long and wholesome life. Specific references and resources cited in these pages reveal specific strategies for all. This publication will help you to:

1. Get yourself out of debt; learn how to avoid debt in the future.

2. Initiate a plan to generate capital and create wealth with low risk and high yield.

3. Recognize your personal attitude toward spending and make a decision to leave bad spending attitudes behind.

4. Learn how to take control of the system and make it work overtime for you.

5. Examine how those with wealth conduct their day-to-day lives, and learn how you can follow their lead.

6. Discover how modern society throws stumbling blocks in your path that may keep you from acquiring wealth. We are led to believe that wealthy people know something that

we don't. As you shall see, this is just not true! Wealthy people value capital the same as do other people. In fact, they are reluctant to part with cash unless they can be certain that prices are as low as possible and quality is guaranteed. Rich people will always select a bargain over a convenience, and they will use every resource at their disposal to find those bargains. In this age of information, these same resources are available to you. They are as easy to find as libraries, and are accessible as free circulars and newspapers.

The gathering and the proper use of information is so important to creating wealth that a veritable philosophy can be made of it. By using this book you will learn how to:

1. Avoid using coupons that cost you money instead of saving cash.

2. Save 50% to 80% by buying in bulk or by buying things wholesale.

3. Barter or trade your skills and services for whatever it is you need without spending a cent.

4. Slash costs and still have quality health care, medicines, and eyeglasses or contact lens prescriptions.

5. Save big money on expensive consultants and accountants by taking advantage of tax-free services and business support.

6. Make the stock market, mutual funds, variable annuities, and investment frontiers create wealth for you.

7. Avoid being ripped off by convenience stores, and identify legal ways whereby you can be robbed of your hard earned cash.

8. Throw away the "pacifiers" that society gives to the poor to keep them in line.

9. Save thousands of dollars every year by cutting telephone, entertainment, travel, research, grocery, and credit card bills.

GATHERING AND USING INFORMATION

If you are truly committed to becoming wealthy, you will find throughout this book a total of 81 ways for you to expand your investments assets and to become efficient in the things that are important to the accomplishment. Remember the mighty oak from a little acorn grows. *__If you do not agree to apply the disciplines explained herein, then this book is not for you.__*

How the Rich Live

Glamour is the word the French have for elegance and beauty of the wealthy people. Fancy clothing, priceless jewelry, suntan skin, luxurious furniture, and elegant homes are evidences of well being, and sometimes wealth.

Usually, there is a wide difference in the way of living, lifestyles, mode of living, places and frequency of travel between the wealthy and common people. Glamour is good to look at, but also it is inherently artificial. It shows something charming, but it really is a distraction. So long as you know this, you can feel free to enjoy the real beauty. Truly believe in what the glamour is showing, and you will remain a poor person indeed. Mansions and yachts are sure signs of wealth. And usually wealthy people live near one another.

Certainly, the benefits of having lots of money are many and varied. A visit to the wealthy family's home soon demonstrates the entire theme. People who work hard to accumulate their wealth respect and appreciate each of their dollars. Actually, they are frugal. That particular characteristic is never written up in the society columns nor is it portrayed on television -- mostly because it is not especially exciting. Such people are extremely careful about what they spend.

Soon you will be making a choice. People who count pennies at supermarkets are called "tightwads" or "misers." To be called a "Scrooge" in our culture is tantamount to damnation! Wealthy celebrities who are not seen in designer clothing and tossing their money around at posh parties are held suspect, or not written about at all.

Neighbors and TV advertising, fashion trends and the latest fads, our obsessions with food and dieting, everything implores us to spend, spend, spend. Actually, we are made to feel guilty if we don't make those ridiculous purchases. And a stigma is placed on being frugal -- unless you spend your money quickly and as soon as you get it, how can everyone else make money off you?

People who become wealthy and stay wealthy are aware of this vicious cycle and have found many ways around it. They recognize that most of our media exists for the one purpose of selling us everything that is for sale, and at top prices! Everyone likes a big spender. Lavish lifestyles often beget lavish spending.

While those who become wealthy and stay wealthy are asking questions, gathering knowledge, keeping accurate records of their assets, and are staying abreast of every opportunity, others may think they are frugal and mostly because they keep so busy as to not have time or concerns of others around them. Most of all, they actually are being frugal. The truth is that your neighbors and friends will see a conservative, decisive personality emerging and they will become in awe of your disciplined behavior and will admire your adult performance.

Ultimately, the decision is yours to make. Any number of the recommendations in this book can save you a substantial amount of money. Adopting the philosophy and tactics espoused here as a whole can make you very rich. However, this requires a change in how you evaluate the media, consider the options of your friends, and view the spend, spend, spend attitude of society. It will require you to leave behind your old notions about how you treat your money and to take on the financial values of the undisputed specialists in this particular field -- the wealthy. Otherwise, your alternative is to continue running the rat race, pockets empty, and to accept big debt and meager savings account as facts of life.

And here's a promise -- you won't have to challenge any of your moral tenets and you can get there without breaking a single law.

Never Be Broke Again

The first step in establishing a different personal attitude toward handling money and wealth is to break away from preconceived notions about spending. Far too many of us spend money in amounts both small and large, without thinking twice about the price of the item, its real value in the current market, or about quality or possible lasting potential.

We don't question the price of that which we are buying at the time! We fuss about the high cost of inflation, but we don't take our business somewhere else. None of us wants to rock the boat. We substitute gentility and convenience for driving a hard bargain even in places like car dealerships and electronics stores. And these are big ticket items! We expect the first deal to be made by the salesman.

That ever-present "glamour" programs us to skim over the surface and take that which is up front, rather than digging for real value hidden somewhere near the back. Not only do we pay for the product, but we pay for the packing, the sales staff, the window dressing, and even the enticing bit of advertisement that got us there in the first place!

People get stupefied by bright and flashing lights, bright colors or sweet music. They will go into the chain store and purchase their entire needs of groceries and other kitchen items rather than go to two or three specialty stores and save 10% or more on each purchase. Spending is not one of our survival instincts, for we have been programmed to spend hard-earned cash this way since early youth days.

This must stop. The rich people don't spend their money this way. You will be surprised at all the ways there are to be thrifty when shopping. Simple little things are traded off for sake of convenience. We will discuss many of these savings techniques in this booklet. We will help you to recognize these old, ingrained habits and cast them aside. Wake up! Leave your poor person's attitude in the past, where it belongs. You will be glad you did.

A New Set of Values and Change of Paradigm (Doing Things Differently)

Take this cue; it really doesn't matter what your current income is. It doesn't matter how much you have in your savings and investment accounts, or even how far in debt you have gone. If you start now to take on the values of a wealthy person, you will, without a doubt begin to grow wealthier promptly. Your state of mind and convictions are most important of all. While your investment cash may be generated in small increments at first, you will observe how fast it accumulates as you stay with your goal. Remember this old adage, "The mighty oak from a little acorn grows."

You have already taken the first step in learning how to recognize all those expensive bells and whistles, the "glamour" of the top-dollar hard sell, as well as how being frugal has gotten a bum rap in our society. Now let's look at some of the other values one might attribute to a person who is wealthy.

Wealthy people ask questions. They do not allow themselves to be led around by the nose. The reason why they know a good deal when they see it is that they are not hesitant to ask questions to learn about what it is they're buying. They know how to determine the best price and quality for their money. Before they buy, they will know as much about the product as does the well-trained sales person. They then determine the best price and quality for their money.

Wealthy people are patient. They don't buy as soon as a new product comes on the market. They wait until the price comes down. They walk out on negotiations. They take the following year's release of a new model car, giving the manufacturer time to assess its initial performance and fix all the bugs. Contrary to the popular notion, rich people do wait, and sometimes a long time.

Wealthy people gather information and use it. Be it a telephone plan, a method of travel, or a new coffee machine, they will research, compare, and contrast with people before buying. They never buy on impulse moves.

Wealthy people work hard. We all work hard, but rich people are not hesitant to become inconvenienced. As you will soon see, this is one of their best secrets. They are meticulous about keeping track of their money and how it is being spent. They are not afraid to go the extra mile, skip over the 7-Eleven store for the bakery, or even wait until morning if the store happens to be closed, may even go without the item this week. Wealthy people respect and emulate other wealthy people. They keep in contact with people who have similar values, and they benefit from knowing and being with them. They give to each other, bartering their skills and striking mutually beneficial agreements. And they are often competitive, but just as often they will follow one another's lead. Each of these values or rules will be treated at length later in this booklet. You will learn how to question and when to be patient. You will be given dozens of leads on researching information, and tips on how to network and rub elbows with the wealthy, as well as how to avoid "convenience" that ultimately costs you bucks.

The thing to do now is to decide to make these rules your own by using them on a daily basis. As a result, you will find yourself becoming more aware of your spending habits and better able to do something to improve them. Your "evil twin" who buys on impulse and allows so many of your hard-earned dollars to fly into other people's coffers, will be stopped forever.

Your Personal Vision of Wealth

As the old adage says, through investing "you need money to make money." And the faster you circulate your own money the faster it will grow. Before you can invest, however, you must accumulate some starter capital. Barring the lottery or the last will and testament of a loving, rich relative, this means that you must set some well planned goals, create a plan, and stick to it. *Before you start investing, draw up a plan to accumulate six to nine months of your regular income as a backlog in hand before starting your investment portfolio. This is your cushion for family protection.*

Create a vision of yourself as a happy, wealthy person which is paramount to becoming one. Lie back and take your time. Imagine yourself rich, materially and emotionally. What kind of person are you going to be when you are rich? What will your relationship with others be like? How will your home be decorated?

Now that you have imagined yourself as a rich person, you have begun the process of eliminating your past as a poor person. If you draw a straight line between yourself now and your wealthy self in the future, you have a road you can walk, jog, or sprint on as quickly as you like.

Now you have a vision of yourself as a rich person. To realize that vision, you are going to have to do a series of concrete things. Also, because you are not rich already, those things are going to have to start with a fresh approach to handling your own money. Will it take dieting? Will you need discipline? How seriously do you want to live rich?

If you are determined to change your lot in life; if you want to be wealthy seriously enough, you are going to be pursuing your vision as if someone had built a flame under you; as if your life depended on it all. It does.

Having been a high school graduate in the depth of the great depression, I fully understand the meaning of good thrift

47

and living off the land. But the tight economy and mode of living that accompanied it was not all bad. We became better managers of efficient living and our respective businesses later.

We learned to reserve a portion of income proceeds for savings and emergency needs of the future. We were accustomed to wearing clothing with holes or patches sewed over patches. Farmers had large threshing bees, silo filling bees, beef and swine butchering bees. Housewives came together and prepared the sumptuous dinner meals. School children walked up to 2-1/2 miles to attend one-room schools, in rain, sleet or snow. Ours was 2-1/4 miles distant. It seemed further in rain, snow or cold winds at below zero temperatures. I chose a pony over a bicycle, though I really had no choice. My pony's yearling colts brought $27 not yet broken to ride. All those experiences and privileges were honorable and served as a superior foundation for high school, for agricultural college and graduate education, A distinct honor it was to be named salutatorian at Iowa State University at Ames in the graduation class of 1936. I immigrated to Seattle in 1968, and established a successful real estate and investment brokerage business. Following retirement in 1980, I met my wife Martha and built a new family room, where I have my office and work area. I wrote 22 books on the subject of investments 1991 to 1996. The last book entitled "The New Investors' Bible" is for use by new and experienced investors.

Cost Control -- Assessing Your Current Wealth

Having decided to leave behind your casual attitude toward the way you spend money and to incorporate into your life the spending and saving attitudes of the rich, it is now time to take inventory. Leave no stone unturned. Make a complete list of all of your assets: savings, bankbooks, checkbooks, IRA's, stocks, bonds, CD's, Christmas funds, piggy banks, rainy day emergency funds, vehicles, furnishings, everything. Bring it all together and prepare to write it all down so as to permit you to understand it in the future. You don't have to be an accountant, and you don't have to list everything in a ledger book. Simply use a listing that you can keep and can understand later. A computer file will do. Start adding assets.

Real estate which you own may be included in your list. Now, set that list aside. We will be concerned only with liquid assets, or assets that can be turned quickly into cash. Then you must bring yourself up to date. All checkbooks and other listings must be balanced. Assess current stocks, bonds, and mutual funds. An exact dollar equivalent must be applied to all your liquid assets as of today! Know where all these items are located. After you sum up all the totals, seriously make a commitment to keeping track of how everything is doing on a weekly basis. Don't get depressed! You are looking at the past. The future starts right now. Make it a game for all in the family. Everyone can participate to become wealthy!

Ask each family member to write down and date his own assets, savings accounts, piggy banks, etc. Initial each item and amounts. I suggest tally sheets to record daily spending by each family member. Let everyone make his daily entries. Compete for the common good and everyone wins.

Make a commitment to updating this record as often as possible -- weekly, monthly, and quarterly. Make it a game for all members of the family. The important thing is to do it regularly.

So-called penny pinchers have been the butts of jokes and objects of derision for centuries; they are creatures we should not want to emulate. We know that you are none of these things. To have the vision and drive to want to become rich is not necessary to become sinful. To be focused and thorough, it is not necessary to even become obsessed or to develop antisocial tendencies. You have a right to know exactly what belongs to you at any given time. The matter is your personal business only and is a private affair, which needs to be thoroughly understood only by

49

you. Each one of us is the hub (as in the hub of a wheel) and the hub of his own universe which goes around him/her only.

When we were very young, a nickel, a quarter, and even a penny was considered to be something precious; a tiny bit of personal responsibility. You went to the store and exchanged those coins for wonderful things such as bubble gum, balls or comic books. It is time to regain that source of appreciation, that sense of value; every penny counts.

Become Debt Free

We are living in a society that goes out of its way to put us in debt. Being in debt is one of the fundamental elements that keeps you from living rich. It is how "the club" keeps its golden gates closed; how the wealthy keep us poor. Even teenagers are in these days! The cycle of spending and owing is distressful; it addles us and turns us into anxiety-ridden compulsive spenders. People are lost in debt, forced to worry about it. Some people even drown in it. There is no choice for you but to leave it; you must get rid of debt.

First, as above advised, you must assess what you own. Now gather together all your bills. Everything that you owe to someone else must be tallied up. Next month's rent; the entire debit on all your credit cards, total of what you will be acquiring, total that remains unpaid for your car, your home, taxes, school, and clothing. Don't invent bills. Just total up your entire debt as they are today. You must develop a plan to deal intelligently with these bills. Start now! Throwing money at your problems is entirely too common a solution. People who are distracted, depressed, or anxious tend to spend money thoughtlessly. We are "cheered up" by self indulgence, be it with food, new clothes, larger tools, or whatever.

But when we think about this, what is really going on is that we are masking our problems! We are bypassing the real problems. This keeps you isolated and troubled. What's worse is that it keeps you poor. If you feel the need for reassurance, apply to a friend, relative, community assistance center, and talk it out.

Stop Using Credit Now

One of the greatest tricks used to keep you from becoming rich is the "buy now, pay later" theory. It is a simple matter to recognize this habit and stop it right now. The average credit card holder cannot resist temptation, and may be thousands of dollars in debt at any given time. Things are purchased easier when credit cards are processed for payment. The bill doesn't have to be paid all at once, but only in small monthly payments. Often a purchase is made that is not really needed. These purchases keep home shopping channels in business. Most of them charge a substantial service fee to the tab. Just for the privilege of spending your own money. Throw your credit cards away; cut them up to destroy them.

If you can't pay all of your bills right now, break them down and pay them off as quickly as possible. Your creditors want the money badly enough to listen to reason. It costs them big money to hire collection agencies or to send lawyers after you; that's why you get so many warnings before any legal action is taken. Contact your creditors directly, in person if possible, prior to their contacting you. Tell them you want to break down the payments to less per month; that you will be sending a smaller payment every two weeks rather than once monthly, until the debt is paid in full. Some creditors will agree to settle for 50 cents on the dollar if you ask for it. You'll be surprised how many will accept.

Avoid Bankruptcy

Avoid bankruptcy and seek help. Bankruptcy is ugly, demeaning, and leaves permanent scars on you and your credit standing. It leaves a scar on your record with your creditors and with your bank. Outstanding taxes are not forgiven with bankruptcy; nor child support, nor alimony, nor debts accrued under false pretenses, nor student loans.

For debts related specifically to credit, contact the National Foundation for Consumer Credit at 800-388-2227. Someone there can advise you on a particular debt situation.

In assessing the seriousness of your debts and comparing them to your liquid assets, it will almost certainly become clear that you are spending too much money. Cutting your spending will give you the dual benefit of being able to pay off your current debts more quickly and to start savings.

This book will help you to do a better job on all segments of family living and budget planning.

Wealthy people are extremely cost-conscious, but they live well and they don't deny themselves for the sake of retaining their wealth. They know enough to look beyond the glamour and find the things they want for the lowest possible cost. They figure out ways to slash spending in every facet of their living -- without their food tasting any worse or their clothing looking any shabbier -- and they avoid debt like the plague. In the next chapter, we will show you how you can slash spending in a vast number of ways. It's fun to be thrifty. It's even more fun to stockpile cash!

Convenience is Robbing You Blind!

WHAT A DIFFERENCE A DAY MAKES. To put it bluntly, most of us are running around as if there shall be no tomorrow. We rise early in the morning and blindly rush to work, tossing off dollars all along the way. We pay for gas and toll fees rather than using mass transit, buy 7-Ups, coffee and bagels or donuts, plus a pack of cigarettes and the morning newspaper. We throw in a snack during the coffee break, and lunch time is split between the corner sandwich shop or diner and buying sundries for the house.

Then it's homeward bound in heavy traffic as the auto

motor idles, using gas more than it pulls under power. Perhaps there is a stopover at the neighborhood convenience store for eggs and a pint of ice cream. A cup of java at home may cost you a dime whereas a cup at the neighborhood coffee shop may cost 75 cents to 1.25 or more. So it's pay, pay, pay. Of course, you do get a surly growl from the cashier and an environmentally incorrect Styrofoam cup for all that extra money. Is it really worth it?

Big business has realized that treating the symptoms of society's ills can be a lot more lucrative than finding a cure. Creating services and products which "save you time* to enable you to get to work by nine o'clock, cut down on kitchen work, or spend more hours with your loving family has become a multibillion-dollar enterprise. And yet, didn't we get along about as well before the advent of the all-night convenience store? That's 24-Hour Thievery!

To put it bluntly, the later the place is open, the more horrendously over-inflated the prices are going to be. Someone somewhere caught on that you will dish out double the cash to satisfy that sweet tooth or pick up that forgotten box of disposable diapers in the middle of the night. Does it cost a business more to stay open late? Probably. But do you have to take on their added costs by patronizing it? Absolutely not! So plan ahead and clear your mind!

Why is it that you don't have the time or forethought to plan the purchase any item at the lowest possible price? Aside from relationships and sex, the biggest concern of the average person is -- money! If you are worried about the almighty dollar, what are you doing in that all-night grocery store paying $2.00 or more for a $1.29 quart of orange juice? The prices quoted in this book will vary from region to region, but you get the point. The differences really are enormous. And when you learn about some of your alternatives, you will realize that this kind of moonlight gouging amounts to nothing short of thievery. Use the following tactics to make certain that these Slurpee-slinging scoundrels never take another penny from you. You are too smart to be taken for a ride.

1. Plan ahead. No one knows your life better than you, so figure out what you are going to need for days, even weeks, in advance and shop for those items at the least expensive supermarket in your area. Take those midnight cravings into consideration. You can buy a two-week supply of crisp nachos and hot pepper Velveeta for the price of one of those oily, wilted, cardboard tubs you'll get at Store 24.

2. Take it with you! Candy bars, sodas, veggies, tea bags -- impulse purchases amount to hundreds of millions of dollars in profits a year for the convenience store industry. Save yourself a bundle by wiping out the expense of the impulse purchase. Be aware ahead of time of what you might want at one point or another during the day. Buy these items at supermarkets or discount houses. Stock up ahead of time, and you will have the perfect excuse to stay out of convenience stores, where you are apt to spend at least a hard-earned buck on the National Tattletale Weekly, just for nosing around.

3. At least compare. Emergencies do come up, but even if you must patronize a convenience store, it pays to have the proper information at hand. Which is cheaper, Harry's Midnight Mart two blocks away, or Yung Soo's Deli on Main? If it's the deli, walk the extra block. It's good exercise, and you're showing Joe that you're not so lazy as to part with more than you have to. If Joe's is the only all-nighter for miles, don't just wander in and grab the nearest package of whatever it is you are looking for. Compare! A manufacturer can impose a price on an item that the store management cannot legally adjust.

Compare!

A half gallon of Tide liquid laundry detergent has to sell for $3.99 because that's what is printed on the label. The same sized bottle of Bold sitting next to it has the manager's price of $4.99. Prices on any item can have a wide range at convenience or "discount" drug stores.

Believe it or not, our culture is one of the only ones that seems to frown on brown bagging it. In Japan and Europe, workers pack snacks, beverages, and lunches in attractive containers and take them everywhere. These people know that the real convenience is in planning their needs and having their home prepared food with them to enjoy at any time in any place. An office-bound luncheon can just as easily become a picnic.

In the heart of the average American city, the ordinary lunch costs around $8.00. Even if your costs are lower, you are spending between $20.00 and $150.00 per month. That $1,400 or $1,800 per year for the privilege of someone else slapping two slices of bread around a shabby piece of meat, probably from an old bull. Think of what that money can buy at your grocer's neighborhood store! Think about how much cash you could raise if you'd simply switch from restaurants and fast food joints to good old fashioned home preparation!

Time spent in line to pay double, triple, even quadruple what a meal is worth had you made it at home, will be time better spent doing just that. Work it into your routine while watching TV or talking on the telephone. You would be surprised at what a source of pride this can be. Concerned that your friends and co-workers will have a chuckle at your expense? Well, you'll have the last laugh when you bank an extra $720 to $960 per year for your efforts.

Also, remember these last figures were arrived at just by cutting lunch time spending in half. What if you could quarter your costs? What if your spouse or children did the same? That's thousands of dollars per year! Do some research. Figure the math on your own, then decide when you will begin. Also, Rubbermaid makes some great looking portable food containers these days.

And finally, if you simply must take the occasional meal at a restaurant, seek the least expensive eateries in any area in which you'll be spending time. Compare menus and avoid fast food joints, and don't order takeouts. Check out the place where the locals dine; the food ought to be good and likely will be at a fair price.

Poverty Comes in a Pretty Package

The people who invented microwave ovens are plenty wealthy, but they cannot possibly hold a candle to the multibillionaires who are currently manufacturing foods packaged in microwavable containers. There is no disputing the quickness and convenience of microwaves. Let's consider it for progress! Paying close to a dollar for a six-ounce plastic sealed cup of Beef-A-Roni, when the same amount of money can buy enough spaghetti to feed a family of four makes you want to scream. "I know! I know!"

A young corporate hotshot must have said, "Everybody's weight conscious and in such a hurry, why don't we cut the food into teeny-tiny portions and put it into these neat, neon-colored packages. We'll give them slick names like Lunchables and put thick plastic lids and pull-tabs on them. I'll bet people will pay plenty for something like that!"

Remember, pudding packs and disposable drink boxes, those lurid double-tray snacks (one side has the cookie-cracker, the other side has the cheesy-dunk), just about any product that contains smaller "individually wrapped" products are priced far beyond the value of the food you are actually taking to consume.

It is important to remember that this is no diet trip against tasty snacks and microwavable fare. You don't have to give up on the food, just don't give in to the marketing. We saw what can happen when you plan ahead and skip the convenience store circuit. Now imagine the additional cash you can save (and divert to making yourself wealthy) merely by taking action on the following tips.

1. Manufacturers are counting on your getting so caught up in the newness of the product, the packaging, and its time-saving features that you will either overlook or swallow the extra cost. This especially true feature attracts parents for items for children and teenagers. Remember what we learned about glamour. Don't allow yourself to be seduced into poverty.

2. Break what you like into components and buy them fresh in bulk. A box of powdered chocolate pudding will generate a snack pack's worth of desserts for mere pennies a cup. Prices plunge when you purchase a sizable quantity of something, or when you supply the cooking or the container full of the goodies. Buy and store up pasta, deli products, potato chips, fruits and vegetables, prepare them to your taste, then snack on them when you like. (A fringe health benefit here: you will be missing out on all those strange chemicals they use to squeeze and preserve the food in those tiny packages!) Stop seeing preparation as work and start seeing it as money earned, or more importantly, dollars saved.

3. Assemble your own array of reusable storage devices. Whether it's high-tech dollars saved on plastic ware, or basic aluminum foil and cellophane, you have an inexpensive army of food and drink preservers at your command. A lot of the new plastic is interestingly designed, with separate compartments built in, and even thermal gimmicks included. Take a pile of penny saltines to one side and a five-cent gob of peanut butter on the other side, and bank the 50 cents you've saved! A helpful hint: If your food storage containers look appealing, decorative, or "cool," then you will be more likely to stick with them. Neighbors and co-workers will be less likely to wrinkle up their noses, and the young ones won't get hassled as much.

Pacifiers
Ever since we stopped sucking our thumbs we have been

searching for something soothing to put into our mouths. it truly is an excitable world, but isn't it interesting that so many of the "thumb replacements" society has created for us are addictive? Caffeine, nicotine, alcohol, sugar, narcotics --- it is as if big business wants to find your weakness and create a built-in guarantee that you will keep coming back to its product.

These substances wake us up in the morning, calm us after a run-in with the boss, make it a little easier to socialize at dance clubs. But they also are enervating, unhealthy, mind-dulling, and worst of all for our purpose, expensive. Why don't you sit down and figure out what you now spend on those various items:

Coffee -- We have already seen the abominable mark-up coffee is given whenever you buy it outside of supermarkets. If you are buying one 45-cent cup, five days a week, 50 weeks per year, you are spending $112.50. Now multiply that by two or three. How many people drink only one cup? And double that if your partner or spouse dips into the java as well. Are you blowing hundreds of dollars a year on coffee?

Office coffee pools can save you a lot of money, but bringing in a thermos of the drink and made to your specific taste, or cutting down altogether will save you more (and probably be more satisfying).

Cigarettes -- As taxes and surcharges spiral ever higher, smoking has become our most expensive bad habit. Outside of items from shops and nifty sales promotions, a name brand of coffin nails will cost about $3 per pack. Half a pack a day? $480 per year. One pack per day? $960 a year.

The purpose of this booklet is not to harp on health issues, but you must face it. Cutting down on smoking can raise a lot of cash! And that is the cash you will need to make yourself wealthy. Nicotine gum, the "patch," and hypnosis all are pricey ways to quit smoking. The American Cancer Society and American Lung Association may be able to assist you in your program if you need assistance.

Alcoholic Beverages. It is a little known fact that wealthy people tend to spend less on liquor. This is because they know how to get it free or at the lowest price! Parties, luncheons, casinos, art openings -- free drinks are offered to respected attendees at all of these. Wealthy people attend parties of their own kind and keep their eyes and ears tuned for potential clients, deals, or connections. They never miss an opportunity to further their business potential when out among other wealthy citizens. Why shouldn't you? By refraining from consuming alcoholic beverages, thousands of dollars will be saved in the long run.

Tip Generously. When hosting a prospective client at an eatery or bar, tipping generously wins attention and respect. Rich people have impressed many business clients by using this technique. Buy backs are usually prepared with a heavy hand or served as free drinks. Narcotics are not necessary, are very conducive to sleep or spending. Seek natural alternatives, cut down, or stop. Turn to the Chapter on "Health," for information on how to save big money on medicines and prescriptions.

SODA, CANDY, and MUNCHIES

One of the richest men in America is named Mars, as in almond bars and M & M's. He has made billions off our collective sweet tooth, as have those warring gargantuas Coca-Cola and Pepsi-Cola. We are a nation with the munchies, popping open bags of popcorn and Fritos and feeding ourselves mechanically in front of the TV set.

This is a form of slavery! We are kept from mounting a mutiny because we're gorged and running on sugar highs! Be honest and tally up what you spend on this stuff in one year: and don't forget to include what goes on while watching television. Even average consumption yields staggering costs. The following tips will help you slash spending on tidbits.

1. Cut it all in half. You've already pledged to keep out of convenience shops, so when you buy only half the junk food

you'd ordinarily consume, that's what you are stuck with until the next time you go shopping.

2. Let your tongue tell you when to stop. Wake up and be more aware of what it is you're putting into your mouth. The human tongue is naturally sensitive to extremes in sweetness. At a certain point it will actually "go numb" as your taste buds overload on the sugar. Do not wait until you are full. Candy and munchies are not made to satisfy hunger; they are made to enjoy! When you stop tasting that which you put into your mouth, stop eating it.

3. Find something else to do. People eat junk because they are bored, depressed, lonely, angry, or tired. Replace expensive colas and chips with seltzer and fresh vegetables. Find something gainful to do with your hands. Better yet, talk to a friend; determine what is bothering you, and take immediate action to remedy it.

You won't find all that much junk food in a wealthy person's pantry. Their shelves may be well stocked, but the bottles can go untouched for months. In fact they are kept usually for guests.

Those Junk Food products are a hindrance. For a wide range of reasons, those who have successfully pursued wealth avoid indulging with most of these "pacifiers." Perhaps you should, too! They contribute nothing toward the good life.

Telephones

Most of the telephone services are tied to credit charges for long distance calls and service fees for information that can easily be located in the telephone book. We call friends, family members, and lovers twice or thrice daily. At the least, much of the conversation on the telephone is time wasted. Some women talk for hours every day. We dial information while our Yellow Pages gather dust in the hall closet. Don't let this careless habit continue in your house.

While it's true that wealthy people use the telephone like the rest of us, it's the way that they use this tool that is different and important. They use the home telephone only a few times daily for social calls. And when they do use it, it's only very briefly for each call. The telephone line must be kept open for business use. Tools are meant to be used in making money. This plan can work in most households. Try it and make the plan work well. Incoming toll calls are paid for by the caller and start with the caller. They can correspond by other means which has less costly charges. With a little research, most of the toll calls can be made free of cost. The following list includes some of the ways in which wealthy people slash spending on telephone bills. Savings made with these tips can be put to better use elsewhere.

A. Spend 32 cents and be thrifty. While none can argue with the pleasure of hearing the voice of a loved one from a great distance over the telephone, we must be realistic. The charges can be devastating. Keep long distance telephone calls short, sweet, and infrequent; write a letter instead.

Telephone calls can be ephemeral. They come and go, and fade from memory.

A letter is a tangible object, to be held, cherished, and perhaps kept forever. Writing makes the contact personal, makes promises concrete, stories repeatable verbatim. Our government offers a great bargain at 32 cents for a letter to be sent any place in continental U.S.A. It is direct, rapid and fun. Don't be concerned about your writing skills technique. Just write the way you speak. Your correspondent will get the message.

B. Organize your thoughts before you pick up the telephone to talk long distance. The telephone is a great tool; learn to use it properly. Plan each segment of your important telephone conversation in advance. By carefully planning before you place the call, you are benefitting your friend on the other end of the line and yourself. All of this leads to a minimum of time your toll bill can build up. Remember, time is money. Note: A truly frugal person will actually take advantage of beepers, answering services, voice mail or even by leaving the briefest of messages to be called back. Do so at your discretion.

C. Learn how your telephone system works and exploit it. Do a little research. Use the low rate of cost whenever possible. You should learn to place calls to friends and relatives during weekends when the rates are lowest. Study your monthly telephone bill. Are you taking advantage of the lowest rates often enough? Check the bill each month for accuracy. You may be billed for calls that no one in your household made.

D. Never pay for information that is available to you at no charge. Find out which telephone numbers are designed by the telephone companies to make the most money for the company (like "voice messaging"). Many businesses across the nation have toll free numbers. By dialing the national toll-free information service at 800-555-1212, you may inquire whether the company you are looking for has a toll free consumer line. Ask for it. Use it and save a bundle.

E. Use the new telecommunication technologies. These days, the high-tech computer hacker types call 32-cent service mail "snail mail," since telephone lines can deliver vast quantities of information so much more quickly. Facsimile machines and "E-Mail" can be used to zip letters, documents, even photographs over great distances cheaper in seconds.

Check out a model for your computer or an inexpensive quality fax machine for your telephone. But the savings will be realistic only if you don't get hooked on those online computer services that come with modems, for a fixed monthly fee, whether you use it or not. And avoid those super-inflated fax costs at convenience stores; $2 to send two pages anywhere in 30 seconds is a rip-off.

Periodicals

There is no reason why you should ever have to pay even

cover price for any publication, particularly newspapers and magazines. Here's an insight into the economics of periodical publication. When a daily, weekly, or monthly goes to press, it is already paid for. Advertising and subscriptions make up virtually the entire operating proceeds of the publications covering salaries and distribution, which means that sales on the news stands are gravy! Every newspaper needs to raise its circulation because it forces advertisers to continue paying tens of thousands of dollars to reach all those readers. This is one reason why periodicals offer such low subscription rates, and that's why you should take advantage of them.

The reason Sports Illustrated is one of the top selling magazines in the world is because the swimsuit issues attract reprint issues. Take a look at their subscription offers in their television commercials. You are being asked to pay up to 50% off the cover price of the magazine that costs $3 on the newsstands. Pick up those annoying cards that are always falling out of popular magazines between September and November. Those annual subscription drives can save up to 70% off the retail price of many of them! Assemble a list of the ones you really want but won't be able to borrow from your work center or flip through at a friend's house. Then, go for it!

Entertainment

You work hard all week and you are doing what it takes to save money. It stands to reason you want to enjoy yourself on your own time when not working, but entertainment spending seems to be the logical area to focus on if you want to cut the fat from your budget. Well, you don't necessarily have to be less entertained in order to spend less money at having fun! Let's see how wealthy people approach their leisure time.

A good share of wealthy people's entertainment is learning. There can be no argument here; the more you know, the richer your life becomes, the greater your potential for becoming cash rich. These people read extensively and regularly. In fact, objective reading is much of their entertainment. They borrow books, subscribe to magazines, watch cable television (but won't pay for premium channels), attend lectures and seminars, and so on, all at minimal cost. Open your mind, too, so that hundreds of opportunities will start flowing your way.

Wealthy people enjoy culture and the arts. Cultural and ethnic centers or events can put you in touch with worlds of diversion and entertainment. If you aspire to wealth, it is important for you to become more aware and worldly. Exposing yourself to the aspirations and experiences of your own and other cultures will expand your sphere of knowledge and keep your mind open to ideas that otherwise would be alien to you and others of your family.

Wealthy people enjoy quality entertainment. Museums, zoos, botanical gardens, public parks, and libraries provide inexpensive and wholesome local entertainment for singles and family groups. Summer picnics at these sites are always inviting for the entire family. As public services, these institutions will often provide forums for classical, jazz, and even popular music. Also excellent prints of contemporary and classical films, plays, readings of poetry and prose fiction are available. Symposiums on aspects of nature and the environment, travelogues and special exhibits are often community functions. You can contribute a nominal donation and receive a calendar of events on the schedules ahead. Get over your migraine headachy school-trained prejudices against these attractions that can change your life enjoyably

Poor People Own Everything!

As you will see later, as you read this book, learning to appreciate culture is like learning a new language. It will give you access to areas from which you would have ordinarily been excluded. For example, a Shakespeare play performed free of charge in an open park can offer you and a date a lovely evening's entertainment. But it also has the potential to bring you into conversation at some other time with Bard aficionados, at a cocktail party or business luncheon.

You've already talked up the soaps or the football game at the water cooler. Now try society's Miles Davis orchestral music with someone in the board room. Live a richer life by opening your self up to the culture and entertainment enjoyed by the rich citizens down the block.

Instead of planning how to engage in a concentrated game of chess with big business, we are taught to shoot a losing game of craps. Advertising and the media would have us run out and purchase the biggest, brightest, and newest as each item comes on the market. We are compelled to buy a product and remain loyal to it, at least until something "new" and "improved" comes along. The jingles, the catch phrases and the celebrity endorsements, "you gotta have it."

The mark of good salesmanship is ability to convince people that they must buy something that they really don't need. An even better salesman has an ability to sell to another person at twice the going rate. Poor people wind up with their homes cluttered with knick knacks and a year's supply of that miraculous spray-powder for hair you're supposed to squirt onto your head.

Think about your struggling friends and neighbors. Isn't it interesting that these people have literally tons of stuff? Gizmos, gadgets, knick-knacks, the latest, the hottest, last year's latest and hottest; it goes on and on.

Why is it that when you visit wealthy people's homes or see them in magazines or TV profiles, their homes seem so sparse, uncluttered, almost Spartan? Are their housemaids that good? Is it all that closet space?

The Stigma of Ownership

One of the biggest leaps to truly living rich on any income

is the realization that you don't need to be saddled with junk. Wealthy people have self esteem. They set high standards for themselves and the products and services they purchase.

For the rich, every item bought is a valued addition to the home, cherished and placed there with care. Luxury items such as electronic equipment, vehicles, jewelry, art, antiques, and furniture are thoroughly researched for durability, longevity, versatility, and quality of construction. The rich would rather have a very few nice things, and this is what distinguishes them.

The shift in attitude or change of paradigm you need to make may not be as big as you think. In order to live rich, you do not need to stop buying things altogether and bank all of your savings. You need to treat yourself to the finest -- at the lowest possible cost. To do this, first of all, you are going to have to take a good strong look at the concept of needing, not wanting, everything you see. Only a very few items of the very best will completely satisfy those who live and think rich. In fact, it is not necessary to own valuables in order to appreciate their value and worth, as we shall soon see. This is known as keeping control. We will observe a sudden and subtle, highly potent, shift in power.

Patience Yields Big Savings

"How could I ever have lived without that?" Well, you did, and it taught you an important lesson. And you can live without it in the future.

Patience is more than a virtue; it places you in the driver's seat and can save you tens of thousands of dollars. A person who is patient, asks questions, and doesn't appear very eager is an anomaly to a salesman. Patient people have nothing to lose by walking out of the store empty handed -- a store owner's worst nightmare! When you are patient, you can go anywhere with your own agenda, your own price range, and take command. You have nothing to lose, because your attitude creates a situation where you can negotiate and watch those prices start to tumble! Following are some pointers on how to apply patience to avoid paying top dollar on just about anything.

1.   Wait for a big sale -- or find one. Having a sale is a company's tactic for luring buyers into the store. Buyers will pick up several other products on impulse in addition to the item on sale. Don't fall for this! Get in there, browse if you must, then get what you need, and leave. Examine local newspapers, penny savers, and even periodicals from other communities in your area for sales on things you need. If necessary, call the store, and make certain the item you want is still available and on sale. Buy the item and bank the savings.

2.   Keep on the lookout for the "sell-through." Often new products are priced substantially lower than established comparable products so that initial sales can skyrocket. This practice is called "pricing to sell-through" and is also used to create a fanfare, build confidence in the product, and to make a quick buck. It is how a thick hardcover book can hit the stands and be marked down 25% on day one, or a certain compact disc can be priced at $10.99 when so many others cost $15. Those of us with kids might recall how Nintendo dropped the price of its basic unit dramatically a few years ago. It caused a feeding frenzy, and now we're all stuck paying through the nose for all those games. Disney uses sell-through to grab the number one slot of videocassette sales and breaks its own records every year!

Take advantage of sell-through if you really want the items in question and don't forget to use the rebate offers these things often enclose. Prices will only go up after the fanfare dies down.

3.   Wait for prices to drop. The opposite of sell-through occurs when a manufacturer believes demand will be so great for a product that a high price will not deter sales. If demand is so great, why shouldn't a hefty tag be placed on the supply?

Once you have gotten over this stampede mentality, you might find after some time that you really don't even need this product. On the other hand, if you decide the item still has merit for you, it is quite possible you'll be rewarded for your patience with a somewhat saner price.

4. Roll-out models, "cutting-edge" technologies, and new, "improved" systems are expensive and full of bugs. Cut through the hyper and realize that "new and innovative" is only so until next year. Technologies are developing so rapidly that expensive items like cars, stereos, and computers are becoming archaic in months. When did "beta" cassettes go? Will digital audio-tape systems catch on?

Those of us on the cutting edge can often get nicked in the wallet, and there's nothing worse than dragging a $2,000 item up into the attic "for when Jamie gets a little older." Go to knowledgeable people and ask questions. Everyone is biased so go to several people.. Find an appropriate copy of Consumer Reports (at the library) and take notes. Like natural selection, the strongest and fittest will wait patiently for the perfect acquisition.

5. Do not rely on advertising alone. The most stunning savings and the most amazing bargains will not necessarily be advertised to the general public. Wholesale outlets, foreclosures, auctions, thrift shops and stores off the beaten path rarely take out television or print advertising. As you will see later, there are many places where real killings can be made. And though they might never admit it, those places are where wealthy people may be found browsing and buying at huge savings. Read on! And remember, you've stopped shooting craps and started playing chess.

Don't Buy It -- Borrow It

Think about the various "collections" you have laying around the house. Books, videos, CDs, audio cassettes, costume jewelry, porcelain figurines: What percentage of these things do you truly prize? Which ones did you pick up because "it was hot at the time" or "the cover looked good." You are wasting money if your purchase gathers dust from disuse. Here are some alternatives. They all do suggest good thrift and are great money savers.

There is a place close to your home where you can find the latest best-sellers, excellent mysteries, endless rows of dictionaries and other references, even music and videos on cassettes. Go there, show them some ID, check out whatever appeals to you, and enjoy it at home. This place is your public library. After you are finished with the loaners, you are privileged to return them to the library, so they will not clutter up your home. Rent it. We all know how video stores have saved families small fortunes (and saved us the anguish of spending so much money). And there are so many items that can be rented for but small change. Carpet and furniture cleaners, floor sanders, paper shredders, computers, VCRs, wheel chairs, business equipment; almost anything you can think of can be rented. Check rental listings in your local Yellow Pages. Why purchase a costly product that you will need but once or twice a year?

Classifieds

How many pieces of virtually untouched exercise equipment have sold for up to 90% off regular cost? Take advantage of other people's impulse purchases. Scour the classifieds in various publications for all kinds of worthwhile bargains. It requires a bit of marching. It pays to know a lot about the product you are shopping for.

Relieve a Friend of It

If you don't have to own it, then it really doesn't matter where you get it from, so long as it's agreed that you will return it sometime. From a cup of sugar to a new record you'd like to sample, what is a friend and neighbor for? Items become currency if they are swapped, and anything that substitutes for cash is good. Remember, the best way to borrow is to offer something first. This can range from saying something nice to bartering an item or service in return.

Take What You Collect Seriously

When it comes to placing something on the shelf in your home, take a cue from the wealthy: Put something there that really matters to you; something in which you can take personal pride, and not allow yourself to part with a dime for anything else.

Think about the kinds of things you keep buying. Make a list of criteria for actually spending money on an item. If it's a CD, for example, then you have to be crazy about at least five songs on the album. If the item does not meet your standards, but you feel that you'd still like to enjoy it, then rent one or find some way to borrow it.

Bargains

TRACKING THEM DOWN. We have all been envious of a friend or relative who managed to snare some kind of breathtaking accessory at an impossible low price. Then there are all those obnoxious, ritzy types who always seem to grab high-ticket items "for a song," claiming "I was so lucky! It was a steal!" He is probably lying.

Wealthy people will go to great lengths to avoid being outwitted by sales glamour. Targeting bargains is one of the main ways they get wealthy and they soon know that keeping costs low is the primary way to stay wealthy.

At the same time, they won't sacrifice on quality. Buying something cheap that falls apart is tantamount to buying it twice, and certainly that is a sin! This requires a little research, a little patience, and a little adventure, but the result is a tremendous pay-off. Here are some of the things you will need to hunt down bargains:

Local "Penny-Saver" Publications. They are often inserted in your Sunday newspaper or can be found stuck in your mail box or apartment lobby. Chock full of leads, coupons, and promotions, they are worth closer study. Watch out for expiration dates and check with stores to make certain the item you want is still available. Community publications, newspapers, newsletters, and magazines designed to service neighborhoods have almost always been tools for businesses attracting local patrons. Special prices may be included in these periodicals which may not be available to "outsiders."

Spy Networks

Your chances of finding bargains increase dramatically when you bring fellow bargain-hunters in on the case. Let friends and relatives know exactly what it is you are looking for. Do not be distracted by the flotsam and jetsam they turn up! You are mining for precious metal of a specific nature, and running off on tangents to take advantage of bargains you won't need will wind up costing you more than you would have saved. Help your friends find something they're looking for and ask that they return the favor when the time arrives.

Plotting Your Course

Get a map. Contact the source of the bargain and ask for exact instructions on how to get there. If it costs you the difference in auto fuel, food, tolls, and body armor to reach the bargain, forget it. Resolve not to be distracted by other sales or baited by impulse purchases. This is why shopping malls and department store escalators are set up the way they are. If you are forced to pass all those others and all that extra merchandise, you are much more likely to purchase something on top of what you went there to buy. Do not let this logic apply to you. Look. Don't buy.

Off the Beaten Path

There are a million nooks and crannies where bargains can be hidden. Explore the places you would not ordinarily shop. Check the telephone directory, garage sales, charity events, church bazaars, thrift shops, flea markets, even salvage stores and the Salvation Army. When you carry your pride within yourself, there is no need to be concerned about any stigma attached to these. Savvy bargain hunters know and take advantage of this. Antiques, too.

Buy in Bulk

This can be a fun project and your freezer will pay for itself many times over.

There are huge depots and just-above-wholesale outlets currently opening all over the nation. Many of them are more than farmers' markets. Housewares, sports, and gardening equipment, even lumber, construction equipment, and cars are sold alongside canned foods and products at sizeable discounts. As with anything else recommended here, compare prices (keep a record of them) and plot your course. You may decide to hit more than one of them on a single trip. You can find wholesale distributors in the Yellow Pages. Do a little research, make room for some extra storage in your handy cabinets, attic, or closets, and hack away at those shopping bills.

Government Auctions

Auctions are usually held to liquidate confiscated property or when merchandise falls into the hands of the government. While quality and variety can run the full spectrum, the remarkable savings potential makes these auctions well worth looking into. It is not unusual for mechanically sound cars to sell for $500 or less. Desirable real estate can be purchased for a song and resold at a substantial profit.

Wholesale by Mail

The showstopper of all bargains must be shopping by mail or over the telephone. You will be amazed at how many corporations and manufacturers will forego the middle man and sell their product directly to the purchaser at wholesale prices which can amount to 30% to 90% off regular retail value. let's see how this happens.

1.   You'll probably need a credit card, although, if you're willing to wait a bit longer to receive your purchase, cashier's checks and money orders are acceptable. It will require patience to wait out the deliberations of dealing at this level of purchase. This is not shopping by impulse or for instant gratification. Delivery is usually fast and can often be arranged around your busy schedule.

2.   Many wholesale sources will have minimum orders or a set amount required to be bid before an actual sale can be consummated.

3.   Don't buy more than you need because the prices are at rock bottom. The best way to determine whether an item you are considering to buy is sold wholesale directly from the manufacturer is to find out who makes the product, locate their 800 number in the nifty U S West directory we discussed above, and ask. Try the customer service department initially.

Barter: The Oldest Form of Commerce

YOU SCRATCH MY BACK. Before there was such a thing as currency, buying and selling between people consisted of swapping the things one had for the things that another person might offer. If it was a bushel of wheat one needed, it might be exchanged for this month's hotcakes. Then that person was located and the trade was finalized. Trade agreements were made in direct response to mutual need, and no greenbacks or gold bars entered into the transaction.

As with any business transaction, the secret of bartering

lies in assessing what you've got and being able to put people who can benefit one another in contact. This establishes a network that will ultimately benefit both of the parties. Close-knit association of well-to-do people like Kiwanis Club, Lions Club, and Free Masons are perfect examples of successful barter networks. Make a name for yourself helping people to get what they want for no cash payment, and it will be that much easier to start asking for things you need free of charge.

Establishing a System of Contacts

Quite often people enter into social situations with strangers and remain aloof. You stick with the people you know at the cocktail party, leaving the strangers to visit among themselves. Next time you are in such a situation, you'll consider that each of those strangers is a potential bartering partner. You'd be surprised. Make friends with them.

Here's an exercise for you. Imagine that you are among people that you don't know; seek out someone and develop a conversation with him. What does he do for a living? What hobby does he have? Does he have a family? What does he need to make life a bit easier? If a match has been made, go for it! Get his business card or his telephone number. When you get home, make a note of this man and how to reach him. Next time the mission will be easier.

Knowledge is Wealth

Information can save you big money. As the information age develops around us, it is vital for us to realize that wealth is born of knowledge. Figuring out how to access data which can help you in your quest to accumulate wealth is three-quarters of the battle. For those of us not raised with an ability to assess both items being considered in the transaction, ask if a person has an extra item, find out what he needs. It may require several barters to come up with the item he needs. Skills and possession come into play when bartering. The person who offers an item first often gets the advantage. By acknowledging your potential barter partner's needs and making an initial offer, you are establishing a friendly atmosphere in which to deal. As your offer is considered, you can reinforce your position by indicating that you have no intention of charging money for your service. You need not ask for something in return right away. This will please the person you are dealing with. Your service will be remembered and the favor most likely returned in the near future. Exchanging services, skills, and items you have in abundance for things you need can save you much capital.

Assessing What You've Got

Make a list of the things you have to offer, such as specialities, areas of expertise, skills in which you have some degree of confidence. Can you sew? Write? Do taxes? Balance record books? Babysit? Tutor? Do you have a successful investment portfolio? Can you organize? Cater? Tend bar? Do you have craft and artistic skills? Do you have a surplus of some things?

Take into consideration all the areas of expertise, business acumen, skills, services, and abilities many of your friends and relatives can supply. One of the secrets to successful bartering is with computers in our classrooms, or digital fiber optics in our telephone lines. The forthcoming information super highway may seem daunting. But those of us who refuse to be intimidated by this data explosion can learn to harness its power and use it to increase our wealth.

Look It Up

The first step in making information safe and earn you big money is to admit to yourself that you don't know something when in fact you don't. Keeping yourself in the dark will only prove to be a disservice to you. So much of what keeps you poor is the lack of not simply "schooling," but education. You are like a person in the desert who trudges in the blinding sand storm within 10 yards of a village but didn't know it was there for he had no map. The knowledge you need to become really successful could be somewhere in your own home!

When you gather knowledge, you are making yourself wiser and more articulate. When you smoothly incorporate your knowledge into conversation, you become impressive and respected. Wealthy people recognize people who seem to know what they are talking about and provide them with jobs. When you have thoroughly investigated a certain field, you can discuss it with confidence.

Pursue your interests with vigor. Take a casual or superficial knowledge of something and turn it into a specialty. Shine a light into those dark areas just beyond your field of perception. If you are not as rich as you would like to be right now, the answers may exist somewhere close by.

Magazines and Trade Publications. Many of us are taken up with the glamour of various occupations and lifestyles. Specialty magazines and publications created specifically for people in certain occupations can shed new light on subjects you're only acquainted with through TV or superficial periodicals.

Specialty publications (such as Variety or the Hollywood Reporter, movies that intrigue you) can teach you the language of your area of interest -- the vocabulary and phraseology that can give you access to certain circles or cliques within a profession.

The Library. Whether it is your neighborhood public library or collections at your area hospital, university, or technical school, these places continue to offer the cheapest, easiest ways to gather solid information. Often forgotten are the periodical sections, which can contain cutting-edge information in the form of articles in trade and college publications. Also be certain to ask for help! Librarians are there to assist you. Also, many libraries offer telephone services that can be invaluable. Check this out.

Audit Classes and Seminars. There is nothing to stop you from attending a course or two at a local college. Many have no fees. Keep up with what is happening at your college. Seminars and film programs, cultural activities, and all kinds of other subjects may attract your interest. Off-campus forums can be both educational and enjoyable. Put passion into your pursuit!

On-Line Access. Purchase a modem for your computer; hook it into your telephone system and subscribe to an inexpensive on-line service, such as Prodigy or Compuserve. Nowhere else is there such lively discussions and discourse from such a wide variety of participants. Many say on-line communication and data exchange will become as commonplace as picking up your telephone.

Consult an Expert. People enjoy sharing their interests, and they appreciate a good listener. Find someone who can be certain to know a lot about your interests. Then ask questions; and many well-planned questions! Treat this person with respect and you'll have a valuable source of experience and information. See more later.

Hard knowledge can turn into keen understanding and even wisdom when it is shared. Talk about what you've learned with people whose intelligence you respect. Encourage questions, so that you can apply that which you have learned into a conversation context. All that information will do you no gain unless you communicate it clearly in a way laymen can understand.

TRAVEL

Plotting Your Course. With the economy currently as tight as it is, travelling has become less and less with the recession taking its toll. So that better.times are here, people are again traveling more and farther. The travel industry is again taking orders for vacations and visits and for just good times. Hotels, airlines, busses, eateries, clothing stores, and a vast array of other industries are thriving now.

Accumulate Air Miles. Virtually every major airline offers frequent flier service through which you can accumulate thousands of free air miles every time you fly with a given company. When you have accumulated a certain current number of miles, the airlines will offer tremendous discounts on future trips, or free trips to any number of destinations world-wide. When combined with air clubs, credit card "air-mileage" promotions, and discount travel agency usage, you can literally earn free airplane tickets within months. A little strategic planning and you can eventually go to points around the world for surprisingly little outlay of cash. Ask for "frequent flier application." Remain loyal to your choice of a single airline for all your travels.

Join Travel Clubs. Check your local newspapers and regional magazines for listings on travel clubs and explorer's organizations. Together, these clubs can book discount air fares, group rates, cruises, and tours at big savings. Many air and cruise lines offer their own travel clubs, which you may join free of charge. Services offered by clubs include substantial discounts on tickets, cut rates at hotels, and restaurants around the world, and even personal insurance policies. Contact your favorite carrier's customer service department for details. If you truly like

78

to travel and do so often, you may want to subscribe to Travel Smart (40 Beechdale Road, Dobbs Ferry, New York, 10522-9989). They have an excellent newsletter that offers extensive information on hotel, airfare, cruise, and auto rental bargains, as well as discount travel opportunities of all kinds. Also, your destination area's Tourist Board or Traveler's Air Society is committed to making your stay as comfortable and interesting as possible. Contact them via their 800 number and get data on as many free and low-cost services as they can offer!

Saving on Wheels. Whether you're driving to work on a daily basis, taking a spin to the next town, or preparing a cross-country trip, there are several things you can do to get the best buy possible on auto purchases and secure your car so that you can be assured lowest possible costs in case of emergency.

Bucket Seating. One way wealthy people pull huge savings out of travel is to establish a direct line to consolidators. Often referred to in the travel industry as "bucket shops," consolidators purchase blocks of airplane seats from airlines and resell them for much less cost than the going rate. Travel agents turn good profits by purchasing these tickets from bucket shops and placing them with others. Your savings can start at 25% off the advertised rates, and savings skyrocket from there (especially if you are flying economy), depending on where you want to go and how soon you need to get there. Consolidators can also offer bookings on cruises, hotel rooms, and chartered transport.

Travel America at Half Price

Cutting Hotel and Restaurant Costs. There can be no substitute for research and planning when you travel, even if what you seek is adventure and spontaneity. No one wants the disaster of mismanaged travel arrangements, misunderstanding instructions, or lousy dining experiences. Consult with people who have been to a place before you and listen to their recommendations. Avoid tourist traps by picking up on local media and going where the local natives enjoy themselves.

Half Price Europe, from Entertainment Publications, 2125 Butterfield Road, Troy, Michigan, 46084 (800-477-3234). Their offer is fantastic savings on food and lodging. Each directory comes with a membership card and coupons; you can apply to more than 1,200 hotels and motels and 1,300 restaurants (25% discount) across the nation. These deals are simply amazing if you travel at all; other books are for special locales.

Health

Secrets to Low-Cost Medicine. The cost of health maintenance and treatment will always wind up being the most costly item of anyone's health budget. The health industry, including diet, exercise, apparel, equipment, medical, pharmaceutical, optical, and a myriad of other sub-industries make billions by taking advantage of failing consumers. Any opportunity to safely undercut the health industry giants is to be encouraged. Prevention, of course, is your best bet. Strengthen yourself and live healthy. Surgery must be seen as a last resort, as costs spiral into the stratosphere at this point. Opt for non-surgical procedures whenever possible.

Setting aside time and space to exercise at home (perhaps with a series of inexpensive videotapes or recorded cable TV programs can save you vast sums of money on gym fees. Joining exercise programs can do the same. Place your name on mailing lists like local nonprofit organizations such as the Lung Association. They often send out special offers in the mail for joining gyms and health clubs free of charge. Free, thorough physicals are often offered at teaching or university affiliated hospitals, where professional physicians oversee examinations conducted by interns and residents.

If you cannot afford health insurance, or your small business is unable to provide it for you; there is another source through National Hill-Burton law, if you meet certain income requirements there should be no charge to you for care at hospitals and other health care facilities which receive federal funding for construction and modernization. Call the Department of Health and Human Services at telephone number 800-638-8742 for more information.

The Eyes Have It. There is never reason to pay full price for corrective lenses, whether eyeglasses or contacts, for promotions at the large chains, two for the price of one, and so forth. Do not rely completely on examinations at eyeglass stores and certainly do not consider them replacements for yearly visits to your eye doctor. Eye-wear store exams should be provided free of charge, and you should be entitled to know what your prescription is when you're done. Do not settle for less.

As with furniture and other products, it pays to go to the source when it comes to eyeglasses and contacts. You can save up to 50% off retail prices on both lenses and frames, so long as you know your exact prescription.

Income Tax

Filing for No Preparation Charges. Though it may seem unlikely at first, and if you have nothing to hide, why pay money to expensive tax preparers, tax accountants, and tax attorneys when you can get most of what they offer -- only better -- and at no cost to you? The government has a variety of free programs that very few people know about. Contact the District Office of the Internal Revenue Service at 800-829-1040 for a complete list of these services.

Forms, Education, and Legal Aid -- All Free. Any tax forms you could possibly need should be available at your local library, post office, or technical school. If they are not, place a request for a special form you need with the person in charge there. Forms may be ordered by these facilities by contacting the Taxpayer Service Division of the Internal Revenue Service at 800-424-3676. Libraries also will often have audio or video cassettes which provide detailed instructions on how to file your taxes.

Free courses in how to prepare taxes for yourself, as well as free assistance in preparing your taxes, are available in cities across the nation. Those courses are staffed by law school and graduate accounting students, who are supervised by their professors. For a list of locations nearest you, call 202-566-6352.

The Volunteer and Education Branch of the Internal Revenue Service also offers free legal service if you get audited. Privately supervised law and graduate accounting school students are given special permission to practice before the IRS on behalf of taxpayers who can't afford to hire a professional. Success rates have been surprisingly good! Contact the office at 202-566-6352 for this kind of help.

Business Assistance

Tap into Free Information Sources. One of the best things about our capitalist culture is that we all want to see business thrive and succeed. Successful business means gainful employment, a healthier economic pulse, and general prosperity. There are many dozens of systems installed throughout the nation to help insure your business does well. Most of these will answer your questions and work with you free of charge.

Get Free Advice from Experts. At the push of a few buttons, all the expert advice you could ever need can be made available to you at no cost. There are hundreds of organizations and departments, associations, and federations whose sole mission is to provide answers to those with questions. These are experts who have devoted years of education and commitment to learning their fields. If they can't answer your question, they will provide you with a lead to someone who can!

Philosophy for Living Rich

As you continue down the road to fulfilling your personal vision of wealth, you are certain to discover that being rich is not only about having a lot of money; wealth has a style, a way of living just being human; a special kind of language of its own. Learning that language, turning your ear to its pitch and timbre, will give you a head start toward achieving your goals. We have already discussed things like prudence, frugality, and the ability to see the system through the eyes of the rich. We know that they value hard work and hold as precious every penny they earn. We know that they look past glitz and glamour in order to find solid quality and good value for their dollar. And we know that they don't make "blind" purchases; rather, ask the questions, shun trends, look for long-term value, and discard what they really don't need.

But what about aspects of their lives? How does wealth influence them as people? Which of their personal values change once they achieve wealth? How can we take those values and employ them so we can better achieve our own visions right now and not in some indefinite future?

Flamboyant, like Donald Trump, or conservative like Lee Iacocca; immaculate, like Ted Turner, or disheveled, like any of those upstart computer magnates. The one thing multi-millionaires all have in common is that they allow richness into their lives. Those people value discovery. They see problems not as annoyances or setbacks, but as challenges. They have little use for fretting, since taking action resolves situations a whole lot faster than whining about them. Most of all, they utilize words and sentences in ways that make people listen to their ideas and stand by when the going gets tough.

Wealthy people know that in order to stay ahead they have to take into consideration other points of view. This is how talent is recognized and discovered, how from small ideas big money comes. Absorb data, take an interest in culture, current events, economic developments, the arts, pay attention not just to the media but to the way the media works. This is the language of the rich! Then, don't just spout or parrot what you've learned. Filter it all through your own unique experience and practice expressing your options until you can do so comfortably.

Create a plan. Develop an idea. Find something that truly interests you and seek our role models who have attained great success doing what you want to do. Meet and understand these role models. Only then will you be able to successfully navigate in the circle of the wealthy. Of course, before any of this happens, you must have a solid sense of dignity and self-worth.

You Are Worth a Lifetime of Income. Whether or not you are pure of heart and noble in spirit, if you measure your earnings from your first job for your retirement you are an earning machine, and it is important to let people know this. Hard work, concentration, focus, and the ability to take action on ideas are all characteristics that make you worthy of being wealthy. When wealth is accumulated, jobs and stronger livelihoods are created; the economy is stimulated, we feel more free to spend more. And, any way you look at it, you simply must feel good about becoming wealthy!

Pursue wealth with passion, not obsession. Fanatics are unable to remain happy people. They actually are self-absorbed and greedy, as opposed to having something to offer. Wealthy people provide service. Believe it or not, much of their action is in giving! Consumers part with money because they feel, to some degree or another, that they are getting some value. The richest people are giving others the best value for their money. Take this into consideration as you embark on your pursuit of wealth. You are worth it! Especially when you make a meaningful commitment.

Give and You Shall Receive. Chalk it up to Karma, divine justice, or the laws of physics, but give and you are most likely going to get back! It may not be as simple as an exchange at the cash register, but when you provide a service, when you do someone a favor, when you have given to a charity, you have set something positive into the world that will not go unnoticed.

Giving something of yourself, with little expectation of getting anything in return, rests in the subconscious mind of the person who is receiving. It lends a positive air to your personality and you will be appreciated in subtle ways. When you've given to someone, you are more likely to be listened to by that person. He or she will be more receptive to your ideas and more likely to do you favors. Give, and have patience. One day, you may ask for something completely out of left field--totally unreasonable-- and watch what happens!

Networking--Speaking in Wealthy Circles

Behind every wealthy person are dozens, if not hundreds, of people who put him or her there. Unless you hit the lottery or a jackpot somewhere, you're not going to get rich in a vacuum. You work five days a week at a small firm and someone gives you a meager pittance for a salary. Work the world seven days per week and someone is a lot more likely to provide you with wealth. To truly live rich, you are going to have to break out that Rolodex and rally the forces! Take names and numbers. Move yourself into a complex network of connections, acquaintances, and alliances. Penetrate those wealthy circles, and gain acceptance. The results will be realistic and very rewarding.

Six Degrees of Separation. "It's not what you know, it's who you know." The line has some credence. The less isolated you are, the more likely you are to be in contact with the kind of people who can help you become successful. Seek out people who are successful in one form or another. Connect with them. Ask questions and listen closely while they answer. People enjoy talking about themselves, and you can learn from what they have to say. Keep in mind, too, that it's more than possible that any person you meet knows someone who could make a big difference to your future. A famous playwright recently said that we are connected to one another through six people at the most. For example, you may know someone who is quite friendly with someone whose brother is chummy with the financial attorney of the President of the United States! It's a smaller world than you think, and networking can traverse it quickly.

Presenting Your Package. There are many reasons why circulating among the rich can be a benefit to you. Studying, interacting with, and acclimating yourself toward wealthy people with give you a first-hand look at their values and experiences. Instead of settling for an abstract vision of what it would be like to be truly rich, you can encounter the benefits and drawbacks yourself by watching and speaking with them. You will also realize that these people are no better or no worse than you are. The glamour will start to fade after a while, and you will find what really sets them apart from others is merely their access to knowledge and how they utilize what other people don't know.

Nonetheless, it could be quite a task to approach one of these people. Economic boundaries could weigh heavily on both sides, with all the accompanying biases and prejudices. Your great ideas, your candidacy for a better job, your basic friendship could be ignored if you are too abrupt or wordy. If you are one who is really worth knowing and becoming friendly with, you're going to need a quick lesson on presentation.

These easy steps can smooth out those initial awkward moments and help you toward establishing a lasting friendship.

1. Listen Carefully!

Just as you want certain things, so does everyone else. When we get those things, we become happy. We appreciate the people who bring us those things and we want to please them. In that way, we can get more!

When you are truly listening to a person, you are observing not just his spoken words, but his posture, mannerisms, behavioral patterns. A man who keeps glancing at your potato chips is probably hoping you'll offer him some. You might well offer him some chips, even though he may refuse at first! Learning what he really wants, and then being able to provide it for him, is the battle!

People are always explaining in little ways what it is they really want. Wealthy people tend to be more guarded, but they can be drawn out with polite questions and a keen ear. Listen carefully, and you will realize that this person has a rare ability; and it is very precious.

2. What Do You Have in Common?

When you have common interests, likes, and dislikes, it become easier to guide a conversation in the direction you'd like it to go. Fortunately, human experiences do not vary much. Respond to an anecdote with a brief story that places you in a similar dilemma. Show how you solved it. Share a bit of your knowledge about something that fascinates him, then ask his opinion. Engage, share and listen to what he has to say. You've begun to build a comfortable relationship without being pushy.

3. Offer Something Free of Charge.

Once you have established common ground and have figured out a bit about what this person is looking for, offer him something of yourself. Being touched creates intimacy and when done right can truly start a bond!

As we discussed in the section on bartering, you could offer this person a skill, service, or connection that might also contribute toward achieving a specific goal. Do this without asking or expecting something in return. This will certainly gain you attention, and you will make a favorable impression. Be certain to deliver, however, or you will end up doing yourself a disservice. Honoring your commitment and keeping your promise will invest you with an air of integrity, a valuable asset in fulfilling your ultimate goal!

4. Ask for Something in Return.

Quite possibly the most difficult step to take is to ask for something back. Wealthy people know how to be unreasonable. They ask for favors; they aren't afraid to ask questions, they ask for what they know they deserve. People can be inconsiderate, absentminded, or just slow on the draw or uptake. They need to be asked. The worst they can say is "no," and that will leave you no worse off than before you asked. Your request does not need to be immediate. Try not to let everything seem like an even swap. This can appear cynical or self-serving. On the other hand, don't keep putting it off. Chances are, if what you wish to express is sitting on the tip of your tongue, taking action is your best bet. Ask. If it doesn't work out, rethink your approach; go back to step one, and start over.

When to Go

Exclusivity is relative. Certainly there are big ticket events that forbid most of us from hobnobbing with the likes of the rich and famous. Private parties are a case in point.

Thousand-dollar-a-plate dinners should be left to those who can bathe in greenbacks and feel clean afterward. But there are several places you can go to network with wealthy people where the playing field is fairly even. Hobbies, interests, charities and culture are shared by all of us, rich or poor. Our love of team sports stretches across all economic boundaries. What follows are other suggested areas for networking. We will consider places where large numbers of people gather.

Trade Shows and Expos.

The most likely places to network and establish connections--trade shows, conventions, and expositions--gather dozens, and some as many as several hundreds of thousands of people, who share similar interests, hobbies, professions and political goals. You should attend some of the events where knowledgeable citizens congregate. Talk with them. Get their impressions of current events and other public issues of the time. Ask them about your most pressing concerns; your views with them. Follow the trade publications in your area of interest. Contact the manager of the organization who runs the shows in your community. Make certain that the subject matter and exhibition are going to be worth the price of admission and your valuable time to justify your attendance. Try attending during the "trade" portion of the event which is usually held on the first day or so, when consumers are not mobbing the area. At that meeting, things are less frantic and people you want to talk to have more time to converse with you. Study the programs, attend seminars, then follow through with letters and telephone calls to confirm your conversations and take action on your goals.

Cultural Events.

Movers, shakers, and leaders keep high profiles at ethnic, religious, and international events or other causes for public celebrations. While they may not be as easy to approach, contact can be made if you have a friendly disposition and a passionate interest in your cause.

Museums and Galleries.

If your background is in history or the fine arts, museums, galleries, and other special exhibits may be the route to take. The more prepared you are, the more likely you'll be to break the ice and establish a firm contact. Read up on what you're going to see at the exhibit. Keep your ears open for general opinions about what is on display. Get caught without having done your homework, and the door will slam shut on you. So, get with it.

Charity Functions.

The secret to gaining access to any charity event can be summed up in one word: Volunteer! You can contribute to a worthy cause by working hard and you won't have to part with cash. What could be better? But being a volunteer doesn't necessarily mean demeaning yourself or becoming a lowly gopher--someone to be ignored. Dress well. Handle your chores with poise and dignity. Interact with attendees respectfully, but with charm and liveliness. Don't be afraid to share ideas, and approach the people you need to talk with whenever the opportunity arises. Practice your presentation until you are ready.

Select a charity that interests you. From the American Cancer Society to the American Zoological Society, foundations and charitable organizations are listed in your telephone book and are on file at your local library. If the event is connected in some way with your goals, all the better.

Auction Houses.

Contrary to their reputation for stuffiness, auction houses can be fascinating places, offering opportunities to see rare objects and antiquities of a kind you won't find in museums.

Motion picture and sports memorabilia, animation in art, doll miniatures, and antique toys are among the many items on display any given week. Anyone can get put onto a mailing list. Do so, and go when something of interest turns up. Like-minded individuals, many of them quite wealthy, will be there.

Societies.

Put away those evening gowns and tuxes; we're not talking about the posh society functions you read about in gossip columns. From Audubon and National Geographic, to the National Rifle Association and the Young Republicans, societies and associations are gathering places to share ideas and hopes. They assembly people with common social interests and actually make it conducive to pitch, network, and barter. These organizations can help you find a job or change the one you have. They provide that group of commonality you need to make your approach and the regularity to take that second shot if you need it.

Societies can be costly to join, but contributions are often tax deductible and nearly all of them offer scholarships. Try to find several that match your interests, then join them. Study their publications and ask questions to avoid embarrassment. Be certain that you understand what you're getting yourself into. Practice leadership skills by participation. Become a familiar face with a friendly smile. Your attitude can result in a firm handshake; a distant possibility can become a reality.

Making Your Money Work for You.

A Dynamic Prospect.

Wealthy people know that money is made in motion. Like huge turbines spinning out electricity or wheels spinning to propel a car, the circulation of cash generates interest, dividends, annuities--more cash. Consider it this way: If you were to take the money you've saved through the recommendations in this book and stuff it in your mattress, it will never accrue any more. The money will remain static, not doing anything for you. Stash the same amount in a savings account, where it will be invested into large, sluggish, and highly conservative products, and your assets will earn a tiny bit of interest. But if you turn your attention toward stocks, mutual funds, variable annuities, and brand-new overseas investment opportunities, you have a dynamic prospect. Growth most usually results in an expanding economy. Our monetary system dictates that we shall usually have slow and slight inflation in a similar rate nationwide. In recent years, the rate of inflation has ranged from about 3% to 4-1/2% annually in the United States.

Generating Personal Insurance.

In these times, the harsh realities of the national economy and employment rates must be faced before you invest the wealth which you have accrued. While certain kinds of insurance--health and unemployment--are built into most jobs, it is strongly recommended that you hold onto your savings in the form of liquid assets until a respectable growth is generated. A sum equal to six to nine month's salary is not unreasonable to put aside as personal insurance above and beyond whatever safeguards are built into your work. *Do this before you start an overall investment portfolio.*

The means and methods of saving capital mentioned earlier are perfect for setting aside this kind of savings, provided you adhere to your choice without wavering. In recent years, however, savings accounts have offered such low rates of return that there is little reason to utilize them to save this kind of money. Generating amounts of $100 to $300 in your checking account to then be sent into a high-yield mutual fund or variable annuity would seem to be the way to go with compound interest.

Your money will continue to gain in growth in these accounts, reinvesting itself and generating respectable dividends while still being liquid enough to get at quickly should an emergency arise. And should you become unemployed or encounter some kind of health crises, this capital will act as a buffer, a distinct rainy day savings not to be confused with your general investment portfolio, which should remain in place for continued growth.

Choosing an Investment.

In the investment industry, a period of five years or more is considered to be long-term. Many investment holdings, after an extensive research period of several years, are purchased by an investor, do well, and are retained in his portfolio for several years. This author has developed a process of investing in high earnings companies soon after a stock split. Then is usually the lowest share price in the cycle.

The stock is then held for a period of time and is liquidated at a near-high stock price following ownership of one-half to two or more years. Microsoft and Nike Companies are excellent examples. Stock price appreciation usually ranges from $35 to $50 per share. One of the author's portfolios retains both of these stocks for long-term growth. As Microsoft pays no dividend, there is no Federal Income Tax liability until liquidation of shares. If a sale is consummated, investments sold in January 1996 will have taxes due 16 months later in April. There are many procedures that can be managed for a substantial advantage to the investor. Learn them and use them.

The Stock Market and Mutual Funds.

Management of your investment portfolio will vary depending on many important factors. Some of those are your time horizon, your age, number of years until retirement, income, risk tolerance, cash flow, net worth, and experience in owning investments: Mutual funds, stocks, bonds, and annuities. Your major objective is to create growth of your investment assets. Knowledge you have about building wealth is an important factor in your managing your portfolio. Investors with but little experience will do well to select "Growth" and "Growth and Income" categories in which to invest for long-term capital growth. Each early January we set our goals as to earnings and investments in our three personal portfolios. Over the past 21 years, 1976 to 1996, we have earned more than 20% per year every year with the exception of 1994 when our net earnings were 18.9%. That year less than 3% of individual investors had a profitable year.

Variable Annuities.

Popular investments for long-term growth are Variable Annuities. No Federal Income Taxes are payable until assets of the fund are liquidated. We now have about 40% of our total investment assets in Retirement Reserves Account. We plan to retain those assets in the Account for the remainder of our lives, keeping them for emergency needs. Our choice of mutual funds in the Account are Contrafund and Equity Income Inc, which are Fidelity Investments sponsored holdings. The history of these holdings over the years is excellent as Growth type funds. Each fund has earned about 38% during 1996. The sponsor is international in scope and maintains a well staffed office here. The minimum initial deposit in the Account is $2,500; subsequent deposits may be $250 or more. Each fund invests in about 100 U.S. companies.

Getting Rich With Upside Potential

As we move toward the turn of the century, a sweeping look backward can provide us with insight and a final clue as to what to do with the capital we have worked so hard to save and invest. Following is a brief summary of where we have been with inflation on some common items used by American families regularly:

	1977	1987	1997	(Projected)
One Family Home	$ 54,000	$115,290	$245,000	
Gas Bill (per day)	$ 0.64	$ 1.04	$ 1.70	
Electricity (per day)	$ 0.27	$ 0.57	$ 1.27	
Paperback Novel	$ 1.99	$ 4.95	$ 6.95	

The Dow Theory

The venerable Dow Theory is a system of market analysis developments by Charles H. Dow at about 1900, and later refined by William Hamilton and Robert Rhea. The system has been in use throughout United States investment markets since its initial development. Its purpose is to identify and measure changes in important cyclical trends in stock prices on the basis of movements in the Dow Jones Industrial Average and the Dow Jones Transportation Average (formerly the Dow Jones Rail Average).

To ascertain the present trend of the market with the Dow Theory, an observer must first establish a definite set of criteria to compensate for the theory's lack of specificity. Unfortunately, because Stock prices seldom appear to move in uniform, perfectly defined cyclical patterns, it is difficult to develop such criteria. In fact, different Dow theorists have derived radically different criteria for Dow Theory buy and sell signals. The stated criteria for any set of Dow Theory signals normally include three basic elements.

1. The industrial average and the transportation average must confirm each other. A signal by one of the averages but not the other is insufficient to yield a full fledged Dow Theory signal.

2. Following a substantial market decline, a buy signal is established as follows: A rise by each of the averages to points substantially above their major lows; then a decline by each of the averages of some minimum length that does not penetrate their previous lows. The minimum has never been established.

Finally, each average must rebound from this second

intermediate low and establish a new cyclical recovery high.

3. Following an extended market advance, a bear market is signalled in precisely the opposite manner: A decline by each of the averages to points substantially below their major highs; then an advance by each of the averages of some minimum magnitude that does not surpass their previously established highs. (Again, the required minimum varies between Dow theorists.)

Finally, each average must decline from the second top to a new cyclical low.

Needless to add, this is but one of Dow Theory signals which has been developed over the years. Other analysts have used different signal parameters and have consequently derived different signal data as well.

Although many analysts have attempted to use the Dow Theory for prediction purposes, its primary function is to identify the present trend of the market, not forecast its future. If the Dow Theory does have a forecasting role to play, it is in predicting the future course of the United States economy. It has a good history of record in this regard primarily because expectations of future changes in corporate earnings and general business conditions are important factors in current Common Stock valuations.

Of course, the companies whose Stocks comprise the industrial and transportation averages account for a very significant portion of the total production and movement of goods and services in the nation's economy. The merger of the two stock price averages into a single integrated system has long been thought to provide an accurate Stock Market barometer. Primarily because of the difficulties of deriving objective signals, it is overrated. Despite its failings, a pervasive cult has grown up around the Dow Theory over the years, and many Wall Street analysts follow the theory on a continuing basis. It should come as no great surprise, then, that when a consensus Dow Theory signal attracts attention in the press, stock prices often temporarily respond to the buying (or selling) pressures induced by the rush of the many Dow Theory adherents into the marketplace. As a consequence, the theory is probably worth noting if for no other reason than to keep abreast of what the Dow theorists are doing. On the basis of rigorous and objective analysis, it is not possible to assign any significant forecasting value to the theory.

Although no work has yet been published on the subject, it is quite possible that the Dow Theory's market record could be considerably enhanced by extending the rules to include the Dow Jones Utility Average. (Since the utility average was first calculated in 1929, the investor of the theory did not have the average available for inclusion in his system.) Stock prices usually respond to sharp interest rate swings--and utility stocks are particularly interest rate sensitive. There are two primary reasons for this. First, utilities borrow large sums of capital to finance plant expansion, and the interest paid on such loans can have a major impact on their profitability. Second, Utility Stocks are relatively conservative investments often purchased mainly for their dividend yield, and constitute an alternative investment medium to corporate bonds. Thus, their price fluctuations are closely attuned to those of interest bearing securities. Because of this dual interest rate sensitivity, utility stocks frequently lead the broad market. and incorporation of the Dow Jones Utility Average into a Revised Dow Theory might well improve the market prediction record. As it stands today, however, the existing Dow Theory is more a historical curiosity as one of the earliest attempts at technical stock market analysis and less a useful forecaster of future market price trends.

Yields, P/E's, and Other Trivia

The relationship between price and value is clear, but is exceedingly difficult to measure. While price can be observed with certainty, no one can ever be certain what constitutes true value. Although it may be impossible to objectively determine current value, in the light of hindsight, it is clear that price does tend to revolve around it. Consequently, several indicators have developed which purport to measure value and thereby provide a reference point for the relationship of price to value. *The logic is simple: If the market is undervalued, buy; if the market is overvalued, sell.*

Dividend Yield.

Long the most popular of valuation measures, the dividend yield is calculated by dividing the indicated dividend rate for the next twelve months by current price. This figure can be calculated for any market average, or most meaningfully, for all stocks in aggregate. In this century, Common Stocks have provided an average annual dividend yield of about 4-1/2%, ranging from a low of 2-1/2% to a high of 8%. At times, investor enthusiasm has been so great that the market has accepted a much lower dividend yield than normal. When yields are very low, Stock prices are, by definition, high, and frequently over-valued as well. The market, then, has nowhere else to go but down, so it is not surprising that, historically, a low market yield has usually been followed by declining prices. Conversely, when the market place is rife with pessimism, investors demand a much higher than normal dividend yield to induce them to buy stocks. Since an excessively high yield means that stock prices are abnormally low relative to dividends are undervalued. The market frequently responds to such situations by climbing higher.

Price/Dividend Ratio.

The normal way to calculate an effective annual dividend is to divide the latest twelve months' dividends, or the anticipated dividend rate for the next twelve months, by the current price, with the result expressed as a percent. A few pseudosophisticated technicians invert the indicator and calculate it in precisely the opposite fashion, dividing price by dividend. The result is termed a Price/Dividend Ratio and, in effect, measures the number of dollars the market is willing to pay for one dollar of dividends. In reality, the dividend yield and the Price/Dividend Ratio are, for all intents and purposes, identical; one is merely the reciprocal of the other. For example, a yield of 3% is comparable to a Price/Dividend Ratio of 33.3, and 4% yield is comparable to a P/D Ratio of 25, a 5% yield is the mirror image of a P/D Ratio of 20, and so on and on.

Price/Earnings Ratio.

Most analysts view the relationship between dividends and stock prices as of merely passing interest. However, fundamentalists view the market's Price/Earnings Ratio with a sense of urgency. The Price/Earnings Ratio is calculated by dividing current price by the latest 12 months' earnings per share.

LEADING ECONOMIC INDICATORS

Stock prices usually fluctuate in response to changing anticipations of economic events which affect the welfare of companies, not in response to the events themselves. Historically, the stock market has demonstrated an ability to presage the economy by six to twelve months. Traditionally declining well in advance of economic contractions and turning up prior to the start of economic expansions, the market is an acknowledged leading indicator of the general economic cycle.

A few analysts argue that the Stock Market might even be too good a predictor of the economy. (As economist Paul Samuelson once observed, "The market has predicted four of the last nine recessions.") And occasionally it does indeed go off on its own seemingly mad and irrational tangents. When this occurs, such as in 1961 and 1962, it reacts to correct its own excesses.

But most of the time it maps economic swings remarkably well and has a respectable forecasting record.

Numerous other economic series also exhibit leading characteristics. The National Bureau of Economic Research (NBER) has developed several dozen series which tend to lead the economy at cyclical turning points. From the overall list of these leading indicators, they have focused on a select eleven (one of which is the Stock Market), which seem to provide better economic forecasts than all the others. These eleven indicators, listed in the table below, compose what is often referred to as NBER "short list."

THE NBER "SHORT LIST"

Subject	Leading Indicator
Capital Expenditures	Contracts and orders for plant and equipment (constant dollars)
Consumer Sentiment	Index of consumer expectations
Durable Goods	Changes in manufacturers unfilled order for durable goods (constant dollars)
Employment	Weekly initial unemployment claims
Housing	Index of new private house building permits
Labor Utilization	Average work week of production workers
Money Supply	M2 (constant dollars)
New Orders	New orders of consumer goods and materials (constant dollars)
Prices	Percent change in sensitive materials prices
Production Capacity	Percentage of companies reporting slower deliveries
Stock Prices	Standard & Poor's 500 Stock Price Index

In the constant search for the key to market timing, analysts have frequently attempted to ascertain whether one or more of these leading indicators forecasts not only general economic activity, but stock prices as well. If such a relationship does exist, its value to investors is obvious.

One of the best efforts was reported by Jesse Levin in the Financial Analysts Journal (July-August, 1970). Based on a study of seven economic peaks from 1923 to 1960, Levin discovered that a majority of the eleven leading indicators, other than stock prices, peaked ahead of stock prices. The best leader was new home building permits, with money supply and new orders close behind.

The NBER defined seven economic contractions between 1923 and 1968. The market generally led the economic turns, and a majority of the other leading indicators led stock prices at every economic cycle peak. At the four subsequent economic peaks, from 1969 to 1983, common stocks continued to lead the economy, with a majority of the other leaders beating stocks at the top two times. The above data taken from the author's personal portfolios from 1969 through 1983.

Broad Money Supply (M2) is composed of, 1. Normal, and, 2. Real (weekly) stock market activity of April 1974 through June 1975. This roughly coincidental relationship with stock price trends has been repeated on numerous occasions during the last three decades, making real M2 a highly useful stock market indicator. It is important to bear in mind, however, that money supply is only a moderately good indicator of future stock price changes. Its value is in confirming the current market trend.

The nation's money supply statistics are compiled in all their dimensions as of each Wednesday and reported by the Federal Reserve System after a lag of about nine days. Two sources within the Federal Reserve System itself.

Free Reserves

Free reserves are a measure of the liquidity of the nation's banking system. When banks are highly liquid, they have a large quantity of funds on hand for lending and are able to finance individual business growth and, broad economic growth as well. On the other hand, then banks are fully loaned out, they are said to be illiquid and are less able to provide the financing necessary for economic expansion.

The connection to the stock market readily follows. Economic growth for individual companies, which in turn provides earnings and dividend increases, expectations of which lead to rising stock prices. Similar economic contractions induced by poor bank liquidity mean declining sales, earnings, and dividends, and hence a falling stock market.

All banks belonging to the Federal Reserve System (which includes most large commercial banks) are required to leave fixed portions of their deposits as reserves with the Federal Reserve Bank in their region, primarily as a safety measure. Member bank free reserves are calculated by subtracting, (a) their legally required reserves, and (b) their borrowing through the Federal Reserve System, from their total cash reserves. The result can be either a negative or a positive amount, but when net free reserves are negative, they are commonly called "net borrowed reserves."

Price/Earnings Ratios

Price Earnings Ratios become distorted during severe economic contractions. Under normal conditions, a persistent decline in prices relative to earnings results in a falling PER. A low P/E, in turn, is generally bullish. The 1930s were an exception. The economic depression was so deep and intense that when the market bottomed out in 1933, earnings had declined even more drastically than stock prices and the Dow Jones Industrial Average's P/E was more than 30. A ratio of that magnitude would normally reveal extensive overvaluation of stocks and would be considered extremely bearish. In 1933 the high P/E merely reflected abnormally low and undervalued. In contrast, the DJIA dividend yield accurately reflected the market's undervaluation by rising to over 10%.

Thus, while the Price/Earnings Ratio may be a fairly good yardstick of the relative prices of common stocks, it is generally inferior to the dividend yield forecasting tool.

Book Value

Still another interesting measure of relative value is the relationship between common stock prices and company net worth. Net worth, or book value, per share is calculated by adding up all of a company's assets (things owned), subtracting all of its liabilities (things owed), and dividing it by the number of common shares outstanding. The statistic is a theoretical measure of what a company is worth. If the price of a stock is far below its book value per share, the stock is considered to be undervalued and should be purchased. Conversely, when the Price/Book Value Ratio is high, a stock may be significantly overvalued and should be sold (all other things be appropriately classified). Book values are often extremely artificial, reflecting only what company managements and accountants wish to put into them. Companies which are absolutely identical in all other respects can have drastically different balance sheets and, hence, book values, simply as a result of accounting gimmickry. What is true for individual companies is, by extension, also true for the market. The relationship between market indexes and aggregate book value has, therefore, always been an extremely erratic one, and predictions of future changes in the former from current levels of the latter is a risky undertaking. In summary, yield is by far the most accurate to use when determining company value.

Yields

The yield curve is a relationship between market yields of interest bearing securities of different maturity lengths. (The maturity is the date on which the issuer of the security must pay back its face amount to the security holders.) The most representative yield curve construction is based upon securities issued by the U.S. government--treasury bills which mature in less than one year, treasury notes with one to five year maturities, and long term treasury bonds which mature in over five years.

Normally, the longer the time to the maturity of a security, the higher its yield. Thus, treasury bills usually yield less than treasury notes, which in turn generally provide lower yields than treasury bonds. This is called an "upward sloping" yield curve.

There are two reasons for such an upward sloping yield relationship. First, the longer the time to maturity, the greater is the risk that the "real" rate of return (the simple annual rate of return minus the annual rate of inflation) might be negative; that is, a "real" loss. The longer a security is to be held the more opportunity there is for the actual inflation rate to diverge from the expected rate.

Second, there is the possibility that investors might not be able to hold a security to maturity. At maturity, the security holder will receive par value. But a sale before maturity for any reason introduces the chance of a capital loss. The longer the time to maturity, the greater is the possibility that a sale might be required and that a capital loss on the security might necessarily be incurred.

In summary, the possibility of incurring losses in nominal or real dollars entitles holders of longer maturing securities to higher yields than those received by holders of short maturity securities. Thus, an upward sloping yield curve is normal and is bullish for the stock market.

Any deviation from an upward sloping yield curve is bearish. If treasury bills yield more than notes or bonds, or if notes yield more than bonds, something is amiss. The phenomenon may indicate an abnormal need for short term holdings by the government or by private enterprise to cope with near-term liquidity problems. Or it may reflect an exacerbation of short term inflationary pressures. Or, in yet a third case, it may reflect a policy of monetary tightness by the Federal Reserve System.

All of these situations have bearish implications for stock prices because liquidity problems, inflationary pressures, and monetary stringency upset the normal day to day course of business, harming companies, workers and consumers in the process, and ultimately penalizing profits and dividends, the cornerstones of a fundamentally strong market. Consequently, while a normal upward sloping yield curve usually precedes and accompanies rising stock prices, deviations from the normal curve more frequently precede and accompany down trends. Strictly speaking, a yield curve of government securities should be calculated using all available government bills, notes (there are dozens of each on the market). While such an indicator can fairly easily be developed with econometric techniques, an excellent weekly approximation of the full yield curve can be derived by relating yield indexes of but three types of government securities: 90-day treasury bills, three- to five-year treasury notes, and ten-year or greater treasury bonds.

Managing Your Assets During a Bear Market

The safest way to keep from experiencing a decline in your portfolio assets during a Bear Market is to not liquidate. However, if the circumstances are such that the time period is prolonged or an emergency develops in your personal life, you may choose to liquidate the most-loser during the current market. Several basic facts should be considered.

Stocks experience a bear market every 4-1/2 years on average. Some market declines are for a very long duration. In 1973-74, for instance, the Dow Jones Industrial Average fell 45%, a grinding two-year slump. In comparison, the 21% drop from July 16 to October 11, 1990, precipitated by the Persian Gulf War Crisis, is the most disastrous of modern market events. However, there is no reason to expect another in the foreseeable future. The recent correction during the past two or more months has about recovered to the market level of early November, 1997.

This investment advisor maintains three portfolios for his personal holdings; two are for stocks and a third is for mutual funds and related investments. No bonds have been utilized during the past 20 or more years. Research is a key to long term gains. Twelve to fifteen stocks are retained in the research file at all times. Posting is done each Saturday. As a general policy, prospective stocks usually are researched three or more years before being placed into the active investment file. Perhaps this practice is responsible for a high success result.

Several important factors must be emphasized at this time. Interest rates are stable and at a low rate; inflation is benign and has remained so during several years; profits remain strong, though have slowed some recently. It's a Bull market until proven otherwise, say some of the older professionals. Presently, perhaps the high volatility is more of a concern to most of us. More than 30% of trading sessions this year have involved gains or losses of 1%. That is more than twice the fifty-year normal. It doesn't bode well. The investment market simply cannot continue to move up and up continuously; we must forever recall that the final ruler is the daily gains or losses of the companies behind the specific stocks, bonds, or mutual funds. In fact, the weak economies of the Asian countries could disrupt the domestic markets over the next six to twelve months. Repercussions are bound to occur. However, stock valuations, in terms of dividends, price/earnings ratios, and price/book values, indicate an over-priced investment market. The context of the strong economy and a very favorable interest rate structure, the investment market appears to be discounting those elements.

Following are four ways to reduce your exposure to market declines: A. Switch your investments from volatile fast-moving funds to steadier value-oriented funds that don't decline as fast in falling markets. Advice: If you have significant accrued gains, you may have to pay capital gains taxes on sales. B. Raise cash through liquidations and wait for the market to decline before reinvesting. Don't miss the market rebound. C. Slow down your purchases with dollar-cost-averaging. By systematically spreading out your investments, you will buy more shares when prices dip down, thus reducing your average cost. D. Consider Bear Market funds that "short" the market.

The strong accumulation of investors buying large blocks of mutual funds is a strong indication that those purchases are going to remain in the market for a very long period of time. Investors do hold mutual funds for long term earnings.

Most of the money sparking this market rise is 401(k) money. That is long-term money that's not going to leave the market. What might cause a reversal of this trend? A reduction of the inflow of funds into equity mutual funds for three straight months; that could cause a reversal of the market direction.

Interest Rate Spreads

A valuable supplement to the yield curve indicator is the "interest rate spread," which is calculated by subtracting the yield of a short term fixed income security from the yield of a long term, fixed income security. An interest rate spread for government securities can be computed by subtracting a short term treasury bill yield from the average yield of long term treasury bonds. A corporate sector spread can be derived by subtracting the average yield of high grade, short term corporate debt, such as commercial paper, from the average yield of high grade corporate bonds.

An alternative to the commercial paper rate is the "prime rate," the rate of interest which banks charge their most credit worthy customers.

The implications for actual future market changes have been just as profound. Market performances over subsequent three, six, and twelve-month periods are clearly superior when the yield curve is normal and upward sloping than when it is abnormal and downward sloping. The yield curve is one of the very few indicators equally adept at predicting the market for each of these periods, a valuable supplement to its excellent mapping of major bull and bear market trends.

Stock Selection: From Theory to Practice

The Synthesis

Synthesizing a single stock selection strategy from the innumerable available techniques involves far more subjective judgment than consolidating the several dozen best market timing indicators into an econometric model. Fortunately, knowledge of the market's future direction, such as we can gain from the econometric forecasting models, is also the primary ingredient of a stock strategy. Even though some stocks are always rising, it is nearly impossible to construct a properly diversified portfolio of long positions that will outperform interest bearing securities such as treasury bills during a bear market. The excellent interest returns available during the last several bear markets indicate that by far the wisest stock strategy in the next major downtrend will be a no-stock portfolio. Proceeding on that assumption, any stock selection strategy should be bull market oriented.

The three stock selection indicators which have been proven to be most profitable during bull markets are based on: (1) volatility, (2) relative price strength, and (3) insider trading.

Volatility studies, in this application, seek to identify those stocks which will fluctuate the most in the future. As a rising market will cause most fluctuations to be positive, it is desirable to own stocks that will experience the largest percentage fluctuation. A very basic characteristic of stock price behavior works to an investor's advantage at this point. Stock price changes are unevenly distributed--a statistician would say that the distribution is "skewed to the right." In laymen's terms, this means that positive changes are generally greater in magnitude than negative changes. It is obvious that gains can exceed 100%, while losses never can.

Consider this hypothetical example: Even though the overwhelming majority of stocks rose in the early months of 1976, an investor lucky (or smart) enough to have selected the ten best performing stocks on the New York Stock Exchange *and* unlucky enough to have also picked the ten worst performers would *still* have experienced a gain far above average. The list of his losers would have shown an average 20% decline, but all his winners would have more than doubled, one nearly tripling. The overall return on his twenty stock portfolio would have been 65%. Very, very few comparably diversified portfolios would have matched that record during the first four months of 1976.

In other words, *in anything but a sharply falling market*, it is enough to know which stocks will be the biggest movers in *either* direction because the large gainers will almost always more than offset the large losers.

Although Beta statistics are a very scientific way of measuring a stock's potential volatility, the simple Square Root Rule is superior at forecasting future volatility. A useful compromise between these indicators, one of which has a sound theoretical basis (Beta) and one which has an excellent record in actual application (the Square Root Rule) is to mathematically convert both indicators to the same base and combine them. This can be accomplished by calculating every stock's potential price appreciation during a 10% market rise on the basis of both Beta and the Square Root Rule and averaging the two statistics. The results, by itself, provides an excellent guide to future price volatility. But even this can be further improved by consideration of other indicators (e.g., Volume Turnover Ratios and size of common stock floating supply) which are also proxies for future volatility.

The result is that low priced stocks with high volatility, small floating supply, and high volume relative to capitalization are potentially the most volatile. Such stocks may constitute a quite risky portfolio, regardless of how you define risk. As we shall see, adequate diversification can probably reduce this risk to an acceptable level for most investors. Those investors requiring even more stable portfolios can simply move in from the extreme ranges of each criteria, selecting medium priced stocks with somewhat lower volatility, greater liquidity, and less extreme Volume Turnover Ratios.

Having determined that a market rise is likely and identified stocks expected to be highly volatile, the next step is to fine tune the selection process. Relative strength and weakness analysis provides a superb time tested technique for accomplishing this task. During continuing bull markets, relative strength identifies those issues currently advancing most rapidly. It is axiomatic that as long as a stock's relative strength rank remains high, its advance is continuing. A weakening relative strength rank provides a warning that the otherwise desirable volatility may be about to occur in the wrong direction, and such stocks can then be replaced.

At the very beginning of bull markets and during the tax loss selling season in the last few weeks of each year, the strongest stocks should be temporarily disdained in preference to the relatively weakest stocks. It is at the birth of new bull markets that some of the most dynamic portfolio gains will accrue. The purchase of highly volatile, weak stocks at market lows will often provide doublers in the short span of just a few weeks.

An additional refinement in an overall stock selection strategy is to restrict actual investments to issues exhibiting unusual levels of insider buying. Besides enhancing upside potential, insider buying provides a measure of insurance against extreme losses in the event the bull market prognosis proves erroneous.

Volatility provides few clues as to when to sell. Both fading relative strength and a swing from insider buying to insider selling provide a timing mechanism for moving out of one issue and into new positions for further participation in an ongoing market rise.

Investors can further improve their overall stock selection by restricting purchases to issues with below average Price/Earnings Ratios and above average yields, eschewing all high P/E, low yielding issues. Even though the latter may provide excellent returns over shorter periods, rarely are they attractive holdings through multiple market cycles. Many studies have revealed that P/E Ratios can improve portfolio performance in holding periods as short as one year.

After a decision is made to buy a common stock, the company's capital structure should be examined to see if an alternative to the common stock is available that can yield superior rewards or require the assumption of less risk. Convertible bonds and preferreds, for example, may be converted into common stock at the option of the holder. The bonds can be purchased at lower commission rates and with less margin than common stocks, and both bonds and preferreds frequently provide higher interest or dividend yields than the common. Because of the conversion feature, which causes their prices to be tightly linked to the price of the common stock, these securities also occasionally offer equivalent upside price potential, but less downside risk. than the common stock. Another security worth checking on is common stock purchase warrant. Issued by corporations, warrants entitle their owners to buy a specific number of shares of common stock from the issuing company at a specified price per share during a specified period of time. Warrants are not unlike market created call options, which give to their holders the option to buy common stock from other sellers.

Doubling Your Investment Earnings
The process of doubling your money is actually quite

simple. However, to accomplish that feat in a specified few select years is truly an achievement to be considered of merit. Specifically, to double your money in three years is only accomplished on few occasions. An important aspect of the endeavor is to plan the program so as to keep from experiencing negative encounters along the way. Every negative portion of the effort must be entirely overcome in order to be able to expand the program affirmatively.

Most Americans engage stocks for investments as a medium in which to invest and thus have a simple commodity to manage and to evaluate at any time. The vast majority of holdings by investors is in the form of printed documents as contracts drawn between an investor and his broker dealer. The broker is licensed by a department of the U. S. Government, the U. S. Department of Securities and Exchange Commission. Over the long term, the company's earnings and worth are reflected by its hourly published data reports at the particular stock exchange listed market. The entire procedure is indeed quite complex and technical. The bottom line is that the system works accurately and keeps punctually current.

Some investors become over-zealous when an opportunity appears to be particularly favorable. Too much price may be paid for a stock. Actually, a negative performance may occur for a time. The back-slide must be overcome as cited above. The holding may end up taking four or five years to double its worth, or even may never double its value, ever. A common reason for the dilemma is that the stock was purchased at a time which was too late for such an ambitious program.

A search for double-your-money stocks may be enhanced through enrollment in the National Association of Investors Corporation (NAIC) and its subsidiary, Investment Advisory Service. Valuable research and educational materials to its member investors can be most helpful. Over the last decade, the NAIC's advisory unit has compiled an enviable track record, beating the Standard and Poor 500 Index more than 75% of the time. Most mutual funds don't match that record; about 3/4 of which under-performed the S&P 500 during the same period of time. Often times, very small companies make rapid gains and, therefore, offer greater risk for gain or success, or even losses to the investor. Can you afford to take a loss, even when advised of the risk involved? Think about this issue! Your use of common sense should dictate a decision.

This author closely tracks the broad small-cap market in behalf of his aggressive growth portfolio. We seek companies with predictable earnings growth and with positions of merit in industries

The tide turns for Value funds. Yesterday's darlings have slumped this year. Investors get suckered into performance. The odds are that the top performing holdings in one cycle won't be on top in the next go-around. Today's winners are value funds, whose portfolios tend to be full of companies with below-average price/book and price/earnings ratios. Such funds have not been stung as severely in the market correction, having been off only about 1% on average this year. Value funds seem a logical choice in this environment. Historically, we got a higher return with but slightly lower risk, so it's like getting something for nothing. Best seller author, Bill Donoghue, believes current portfolio performance trends indicate value funds have value. Value fund managers tend to be individual stock pickers, and they will have more success now than those who screen for companies with accelerating earnings. Someone who is selective can find opportunities, and with rising interest rates, it will be difficult for growth funds to succeed. Another fund manager builds his portfolio to reduce interest rate and market risk. A suggestion for value funds is that they are better suited for tax-deferred retirement accounts than taxable accounts, due to their higher rates of current taxable income, compared with capital-gains-oriented growth funds.

Positive economic fundamentals in global growth and inflation outweigh the geopolitical wildcards. For investors seeking a mainstream international fund, Warburg, Pincus International Equity has performed well in past down markets, and returned 32% to shareholders for the 12th month ending June 30, 1994.

The real role of bonds in a diversified portfolio for a long-term use is to offset the risk of stocks. Short-term bonds offer 90% of the return of intermediate bonds with much less risk. Doing nothing is the most costly strategy of any.

INVESTMENT CONSIDERATIONS

The author meets with 30 families quarterly to assist them in whatever is pertinent to them at the time on a planned schedule. Their record books on investments must be up to date, sons and daughters of majority age may join them, and they must have several well thought out questions ready to discuss. No remuneration is expected by the author. This is one great service he willingly offers to people in need of counselling. It is gratifying to have new and young investors participate in this on-going program.

On a similar schedule, you should sit down and review many of the factors which I consider to be of prime importance. Hopefully you can allow some time for this. I want to congratulate you for having a portfolio and an interest in the subject to become proficient to manage your own account.

It is always a MUST to have a full understanding of the position of investments in relation to the general market--long term, where the market is now and what the immediate and long term future prospects are. For example, we experienced a rather active market during several months previous to mid 1990. The trend gradually declined during the last half of 1990, and now may decline somewhat lower. The outlook for 1991 and beyond is favorable; the extent and length of this recession will substantially affect the rate of recovery. The possibility of war may influence it materially.

I have always followed the daily Stock Market reports and also read pertinent articles on important developments for the day. We subscribe to the Seattle morning Post Intelligencer, which always has a good business section.

For investments which we presently own, I keep a daily record on market value, amount of change, when and amount of dividends to be paid, and other vital facts for the entire portfolio. I also daily follow several additional companies' stocks in the same manner. Therefore, when a liquidation of one investment is made, I am already knowledgeable and ready to purchase a replacement investment. Thus, no capital is left idle. Factors included in this paragraph are the most important of all considerations.

Inasmuch as this familiarity is ever present, I am always ready for my broker's telephone calls. He calls at least weekly and our conversation is 15 or more minutes. I let him set the time period and when to call as he is usually very busy. He sometimes calls before 7:00 a.m. I consider our rapport with him to be valuable. He is more than our consultant; he also is a good friend.

We purchased our entire portfolio during the last six months; therefore, we shall remain in a liquidation mode only now, except we consider The Boeing Company to be our best Growth Stock and plan to purchase additional stock when price is $45 or less. It has but $1.00 per share dividend annually; however, it has its greatest potential in growth, as it has had a stock split of 3 for 2 shares at least once annually for several years. This means that it has gained 50% annually. We plan to keep all Boeing stock three or more years as the Company has under contract more than six years of work orders and more are acquired weekly. Others which have a strong potential for growth if recently purchased, or if purchased soon, include: Mutual Funds in Delaware Group; October 11. Value and Invest (Income) Common Stocks in General Electric, Interface

Company, Microsoft Company, Nike Company, Imunex Company, Pacific Car and Foundry Company (PacCar).

A PRACTICAL EXAMPLE ANALYSIS

ABC Company Example Analysis is a good indication of the influence of time on a good active program, and the advantages of deferred tax due date. As date of liquidation was early in 1991, the tax due date for Capital Gain earnings is April 15, 1992, 15-1/2 months later. Details of Analysis of the Growth Fund follows:

Date	Bought Data: Begin	Shares Earned From Div.	Shares From Cap. Gain Distr.	Sold Data; Final	Total Shares Earned	Sold Date Share Value
	Per Share					
1-02-85	$17.625				400.000	
2-16-85		8.500			408.500	
6-15-85			162.0		570.500	
2-16-86		12.123			582.623	
6-15-86			232.0		814.623	
2-16-87		17.310			831.933	
6-15-87			332.0		1,163.933	
2-16-88		24.733			1,188.666	
6-15-88			474.0		1,662.666	
2-16-89		35.330			1,697.996	
6-15-89			678.0		2,375.996	
2-16-90		50.488			2,426.484	
6-15-90			970.0		3,396.484	
1-02-91				$78.875		
				Per Share		
Totals		148.484	2,848			

GROSS SALE VALUE - $267,897.67
INVESTMENT COST - 7,050.00
GROSS PROFIT - $260,847.67

SHARES COMPOSITE SUMMARY
FROM

BEGIN	DIV. EARNED	CAPITAL GAINS	SOLD TOTAL
400.0	148.484	2848.0	3396.484

BUY - 400 X .29 = $116.00
SELL - 3,396.484 X .16 = 543.44
TOTAL BROKER FEE = 659.44

CONTINUED (SEE NEXT PAGE FOR NARRATIVE)

116

A PRACTICAL EXAMPLE ANALYSIS
SOLUTION SEGMENT

A.   Ownership of ABC Company Common Stock was held for six years.

B.   Dividend Earnings are income and are taxable annually. Total amount of dividends received over the six years of ownership is equivalent to 50.488 shares value at issue dates annually.

C.   Total growth from capital gain distributions was 2848.0 shares and per share value on liquidation date at $78.875 per share, or $267,897.67 total. The amount of capital gain earned during the period of six years of ownership, together with the amount of tax due thereon, was paid to Internal Revenue Service not later than April 15, 1992.

D.   A total of 3,396.484 shares were owned at time of liquidation.

E.   Gross value of all shares earned at time of liquidation was $267,897.67.

F-1.   Proceeds from dividends earned are taxable income and payable annually by April 15 following year earned.

F-2.   Proceeds from capital gains distributions were determined on 1-2-91 which was date of liquidation; taxes thereon are due April 15, 1992, which is date following year of liquidation. Therefore, the investor, in this situation, has use of the fund until tax due date, or 15-1/2 months.

Total of 2848.0 shares were earned from capital gains and valued at $78.875 per share for a total value of $224,636.00 was reported earned.

Capital gains distributions are reported to IRS (following year earned) by brokerage. It is then the responsibility of the investor to also report a like amount of capital gains earned for the same year. So, in summary, both the brokerage and the investor must report such facts to the IRS.

G.   Brokerage Fees:

117

Records are kept by all segments of the Investment Industry in the United States as are the records in banks.

Brokerage fee for 400 shares bought at .29 = $116.00 (for purchase fee).
Brokerage fee for 3,396.484 shares at .16 = 543.44 (for liquidation fee).
Brokerage total commission $659.44 (total brokerage fee).

The initial brokerage fee was debited to the investors account and credited to the brokerage account.

The liquidation transaction likewise debited the investor's account and credited the brokerage account for the amount of the brokerage commission.

Each transaction was performed at the respective times when the Buy and Sell Orders were processed by the broker or investment counselor on behalf of the broker. No money actually changes hands; the entire transactions are performed by use of debits and credits as explained here.

The Boeing Company, Inc., has for the past several years issued a dividend of $0.25 per share quarterly and a 2 for 3 (50%) stock split once annually. Boeing has more than four years of contracted orders for new aircraft production. The company has constructed two new plants in the Seattle area recently and is now producing more planes per month than ever before in its history of aircraft manufacturing.

Microsoft, Inc., also is located in the Seattle area and is a leader in the computer manufacturing and research industry. The company has annually paid a small dividend to its stockholders and once annually it issued a 1 for 1 (100%) stock split when the stock gets to approximately $125 per share. Its price was $110.50 on Tuesday, March 5, 1991. There are numerous other fine companies in the U. S. with similar history and potentially as strong profit yielding companies.

THE 1997 MARKET LANDSLIDE

The 1997 investment market has been mostly a rocky experience. Some cautious individual investors have weathered the storms of the market gyrations exceedingly well with but slight decline in portfolio value. It is indeed gratifying to experience a positive performance at such period in our national economy.

Two significant features stand out and have been effective factors in stabilizing the market throughout 1997 to date. Interest rates remain stable, bonds remain weak, and commodities had a severe decline in prices in May, June and July. Now may be considered to be critical in the World Investment Market as Japan and other Pacific Rim nations continue extremely stagnant.

This author's three personal portfolios show strength and stability for 1997. The following data indicate the percent of growth for 1997 to November 24, 1997: Stocks - 34.71%; Bonds - None; Mutual funds - 386.76%. Mutual funds holdings were positioned into money market in early October, 1997, and remain there. The money market entities are stable and have prospect of earning 7.46% on an annual basis.

GLOSSARY OF TERMS AND LANGUAGE UNIQUE TO INVESTORS

The Glossary and Language comprise definitions and explanations of words used throughout the text of The New Investor's Bible. Basic investment principles, philosophies, and procedures which are common to investors of America are described here for your reference and use.

Accrued interest: Interest earnings accumulated on a financial interest-bearing asset.

Adjusted gross income (AGI): Gross income (total income) minus any allowable adjustments to income.

Affinity credit card: A card issued by a nonbank group or organization to its members, in an arrangement with a bank.

Agencies: Securities issued by such federal agencies as the Federal Land Banks, Federal National Mortgage Association, Government National Mortgage Association and the Tennessee Valley Authority.

Aggressive growth stock fund: A mutual fund in which the portfolio of securities consists mostly of stocks that are expected to appreciate in value in the very near future.

All-Signature account: An account owned by two or more persons arranged so that signatures of all joint owners are required for transactions.

Amortize: To reduce a debt through regular and equal payment.

Annual percentage rate (APR): The cost of credit over a full year, expressed as a percentage, reflecting all costs of the loan as required by the Truth in Lending Act.

Annual rate: The rate of interest to be paid over a full year.

Annual yield: The interest rate paid over a full year compounded.

Annuity: A guaranteed income for life, with payments received at regular intervals; a type of investment offered by insurance companies.

Appreciation: A term synonymous with price improvements or advance--a major objective of investment.

Arbitration: An agreement between two parties that a dispute will be settled by a third party, and that the decision of the third party will be binding on both disputants.

Arrears: Amount due and unpaid.

Assets: Any owned properties or rights that are available for the payment of an obligation. They include cash and readily marketable securities held as investments, other items considered the equivalent of cash, accounts receivable, merchandise inventory, etc.

Assets mix: Refers to ingredients of assortment of Investment Holdings held together as in a portfolio or investment index.

Assets summary: A discussion or verbal review of inclusions of a given group of investments.

ATM: Abbreviation for automated teller machines, which are computer-controlled terminals located on bank premises or elsewhere, through which customers of financial institutions make deposits, withdrawals, or other transactions as they would through a bank teller.

Auction: The sale of Treasury securities by the U. S. Treasury on a bid basis.

Balance sheet: A statement showing the nature and amount of a company's assets, liabilities, and capital on a given date.

Balloon payment: A large extra payment that may be charged at the end of a loan or lease.

Banker's acceptances: Future claims on a bank backed by the bank's customer; they enable the bank to finance the customer's business transactions, such as a shipment of goods by a third party.

Bankruptcy: An individual's status in which a state law usually allows the individual's creditors to claim his or her assets for repayment of debts (with certain assets or a portion thereof excepted).

Bear Market: A general trend of declining value of an Investment Market.

Bearer Bond: A bond that does not have the owner's name registered on the books of the issuing company or on the bond. Interest and principal are payable to the holder. Endorsement is not required on transfers.

Blue chip companies: Large and fairly stable companies that have demonstrated consistent earnings and usually have long-term growth potential.

Bond: A special kind of promissory note that represents the issuer's pledge to pay back the principal on a certain date of maturity, at face value. Until that date, the issuer promises to pay an amount of money, usually every six months, at a fixed rate that is determined when the bond is issued. Unlike a stockholder, a bondholder does not share in profits or losses of the issuer or take part in business decisions.

Book-entry form: A way of recording ownership of Treasury securities, in which the Treasury merely establishes an account in the name of the buyer of the securities. The purchaser receives a receipt and a statement of account.

Broker: A person engaged for a commission or fee, in bargaining or negotiating between two or more parties for agreements, purchases, or sales.

Broker's holding account: An account held by a broker for his client and which may be utilized by the client at any time. The account holdings usually accrue at nominal earnings during the time such holdings remain in the account.

Brokerage house: A firm, often a member of a stock exchange, that handles the public's orders to buy and sell securities. The firm charges a fee for this service.

Bull Market: An investment market which has experienced positive growth or which has a reasonably strong opportunity of continuing affirmatively due to the performance of the vast majority of the companies of the nation.

Buying on the margin: Buying stock by making a down payment instead of paying the full price of the stock. The down payment is expressed as a percentage of the full price and is set by the Federal Reserve Board.

Call feature: The right of an issuer of bonds to retire the debt prior to maturity.

Call protection: The specific period of time during which a callable securities issue cannot be recalled.

Call provision: A provision which gives its holder the option to buy stock at a fixed price, within a specified length of time, from the writer or seller. Calls are purchased by those who think the stock price may rise.

Callable bonds: A provision in a bond document that gives the issuer the right to buy back the bonds from holders at the face amount before the date of maturity.

Capital gain: A gain or profit derived from the sale or exchange of a capital asset.

Cash management account: A form of investment offered by larger brokerage firms and investment companies.

Ceiling interest rate: The maximum rate of interest allowed by law or official regulations.

Certificate of deposit (CD): A form of time deposit issued by depository institutions that cannot be withdrawn before a specified maturity date without being subject to an interest penalty.

Checking account: A deposit account upon which checks can be written to withdraw funds.

Closed-end: Companies in which there is a set number of shares which are to be sold, and ar outstanding. The shares are traded on the major exchanges.

Closing costs: Fees payable immediately before you receive title to your home. These fees include costs associated with the attorney, preparing and filing the mortgage, taxes, title search, credit report, survey, insurance, etc.

Collateral: Something of value pledged to assure repayment of a loan and subject to seizure if the loan is not repaid.

Collateral trust bond: A bond that is secured by financial assets, such as notes receivable and accounts receivable.

Co-Maker (or co-signer): An individual with a good credit rating who signs the note of another person to provide additional security for that person's loans.

Commercial paper: Short-Term, unsecured promissory notes (IOUs) issued by well-known and well-regulated business firms.

Commission: The broker's fee for handling a stock transaction.

Commodities market: A market in which there is active trading of twenty-five or so commodities, many of which are agriculture products such as corn, cotton, and soybeans. The commodity itself is not traded. What *is* traded are contracts for the future delivery of these products at a specific price.

Common stocks: Securities representing an ownership interest in a corporation and carrying specified rights for the owner.

Competitive bid: An offer to buy Treasury securities in which the prospective purchaser states the rate of interest or yield that he or she is willing to accept.

Composite return: Dividends plus expected appreciation.

Compounded interest: Interest earned on interest already paid on the invested principal when it is left to accumulate with the principal.

Compounding: Computing the new principal figure by using as a base both the previous principal and change by added interest accruing to the previous principal each time.

Consumer-type certificates: A certificate of deposit with no federal minimum denomination issued by depository institutions for periods of from three months to five years.

Contingent monetary receipts: Money or income that an

individual may or may not receive, depending on future developments.

Corporate bonds: Interest-bearing debt instruments or IOUs issued by a business corporation.

Coupon bond: A bond with interest coupons attached. Coupons are clipped as they come due and are presented by the holder to the paying agent for payment of interest.

Coupon interest rate: The interest rate specified on a bond certificate and on interest coupons attached to a bond.

Coupon yield: The interest rate specified on the securities (notes or bonds). This is also referred to as the coupon rate.

Credit: The promise to pay in the future in order to buy in the present.

Credit history: The record of how a person has borrowed and repaid debts.

Credit scoring history: A statistical system used to rate credit applicants according to various characteristics related to credit-worthiness.

Creditor: One who lends money or permits another person to owe money to him or her.

Cumulative: A feature of a preferred stock indicating that if dividends are not paid in full, the accumulations must be paid in the future before any dividends can be paid on the common stock. When stock is noncumulative, the corporation is not obligated to make up unpaid dividends.

Debenture: An unsecured, long-term certificate of debt issued by a company against its general credit rather than against a specific asset or mortgage.

Debit card: A plastic card, similar in appearance to a credit card, that customers may use to make purchases through a point of sale terminal. The machine-readable card allows immediate withdrawal from the customer's checking or savings account with the money being transferred to the merchant's account.

Debt service: Interest requirements plus stipulated payments of principal on outstanding debt.

Default: Failure to perform a contract obligation, particularly the payment of principal or interest on a bond or note at a stated date.

Delinquent: A debtor who is behind in making payments on a debt and has made no satisfactory arrangement with the lender.

Depository institutions: Commercial banks, savings and loan associations, mutual savings banks, savings banks, and credit unions.

Direct deposit: A system in which the employee's or investor's earnings are deposited directly to his or her account at a depository institution.

Discount: A bond selling below par.

Discount a note: The lender deducts the interest amount from the face value of the note and remits the remainder to the borrower.

Discount loan: A loan in which there is a deduction from principal for interest and finance charges at the time a loan is made.

Discount rate: The rate of interest that Federal Reserve banks charge financial depository institutions that wish to borrow funds from these banks.

Discounted price: The actual dollar amount that the purchases pays for a Treasury bill. The difference between this discounted price and the face value of the bill--assuming the bill is held to maturity--is called the discount.

Disposable income: Take-home pay or net pay.

Diversification: Spreading investments among difference companies and institutions in different fields.

Dividend rate: The annual rate of interest paid on passbook savings account.

Dividend yield: Percentage earning on stocks that can be computed by simply dividing the annual dividend by the market price of the stock.

Dividends: Earnings on the ownership of stock, both common and preferred.

Dollar-Cost Averaging: An average cost of investing the same amount of assets at regular intervals for a period of time. As the market value of an entity fluctuates, more units of the investment can be purchased when the price per unit is lower and less units of the entity can be purchased when the price per unit is up.

Dow-Jones industrial average: Number indicators of the movements of prices of certain groups of thirty stocks (utilities, industrials, transportation, and composite) on the New York Stock Exchange.

Durable goods: Manufactured products capable of long use, such as refrigerators, automobiles, and various household appliances.

Early withdrawal penalty: A fee that the depositor must pay in order to withdraw funds from the certificate of deposit before its maturity.

Economy strategy: A detailed plan for meeting a goal or goals of the general affairs of a governing body.

Equities: Common or preferred stock in a corporation.

Equity Strategy:

Estate: A person's ownership and/or interest in all forms of property. Also, the financial resources and personal assets left upon the person's death.

Eurodollar: Deposits denominated in U. S. dollars at banks and other financial institutions outside the United States.

Exchange Rate Value: The value of a currency of one nation in relation to the value of a currency of another nation, at a specified time.

Exchange Rate Activity: Movement of currency of a particular nation in relation to currency of another nation at a particular time.

Executor: An individual appointed in a will and approved by a probate court to administer the disposition of an estate according to directions in the will.

Face value: For insurance, face value is the dollar value that expresses coverage limits. It appears on the front of the policy. For a bond, the value that appears on the face of the bond, the amount the issuing company promises to pay at maturity. It is not an indication of market value.

Family of funds: A number of mutual funds managed by the same investment company, with each fund specializing in a different kind of security or investment product.

Finance charge: The cost of a loan in dollars and cents as defined by the Truth in Lending Act. The interest charged is just one component of the finance charge.

Financial plan: An orderly schedule of capital movement.

Financial instrument: Any written document or contract having monetary value or showing a monetary transaction.

First mortgage: A legal instrument that given a creditor a claim against an owner's right in real property prior to a claim of all other creditors.

Fixed expenses: Expanses such as monthly rent or mortgage payments that must be paid at regular intervals, in set amounts, and do not vary with activity.

Fixed rate certificate of deposit: A certificate of deposit on which the annual interest rate is contractually fixed until maturity.

Float: Checkbook money that for a period of time appears on the books of both the check writer and the check receiver due to the normal lag in the check collection process.

Foreclose: A creditor sells property in the possession of the debtor with a view toward applying the proceeds to the liquidation or reduction of the debt.

Futures contract: A legally signed agreement for a specified amount of capital at a particular date or period of time. The activity shall be in the "Futures Trading Market" for commodities.

Garnishee: A legal action taken by a creditor to secure payment of a debt by attaching the debtor's salary or other income.

General obligation bonds: Government bonds secured by the full faith, credit, and taxing power of the issuing unit.

"Ginnie Maes:" A name given to certificates issued by the Government National Mortgage National Association, a federally-chartered corporation.

GNP: Gross National Product. The total monetary value of all final goods and services produced in a country during one year.

Governments: A term given to all securities issued by the U.S. Treasury.

Grace period: The period between the date an item is charged on credit or a billing is received, and the date that interest charges begin.

Growth: Appreciation or increase in value.

Hedge: Protection against a potential investment loss by making a counter-balancing transaction.

Holdings: Property owned as of stock or bonds owned by an investor.

Home equity: The difference between the fair market value of your home and your outstanding mortgage balances.

Impulse buying: Unplanned buying or buying on a sudden decision.

Income maintenance programs: Government programs that provide financial assistance to people who need a supplement to their income.

Income stock fund: A mutual fund in which the portfolio consists mostly of stocks noted for producing generous dividends.

Inflation: A period of persistent rises in the general price level.

Installment loan: A loan repaid in two or more payments made at regular intervals over a period of time.

Institutional investor: A purchaser or seller of securities who acts on behalf of an institution, such as a pension fund, trust fund, mutual fund, or insurance company.

Interest rate: The price in percentage form paid for credit on the privilege or borrowing money.

Inventory: A completed listing of all the household's assets.

Investment management: The guiding or directing the management of property such as investments held for growth.

Investment objective: The goal for a holding or anticipated plan for growth of an investment holding.

Investment policy: An investment plan or objective.

Investment trusts: Any firm that takes its capital and invests it in other companies.

Joint tenancy with right of survivorship account: An account owned by two or more persons arranged so that if one joint tenant dies, the surviving tenants continue to have the same rights to the account as they had previously.

"Junk bonds:" "High yield," low grade bonds that are rated as speculative by the major rating agencies, and are therefore considered more risky than high- or investment-grade bonds.

Leveraging: The act of buying income-producing assets such as stocks, bonds, or real estate with a relatively modest amount of the buyer's own funds and a significant amount of funds from other sources.

Liquid assets: All real and personal property owned by a person or household that can easily be converted into cash at a readily determinable fair price.

Liquid Investment: Investment assets that can readily be converted into cash.

Liquidity: The ease with which an asset can be converted into cash with little risk of loss of principal.

Loan provision: A clause in the policy that explains how the policy holder can borrow up to the total accumulated cash value of the policy.

Logo: A symbol used by a particular firm or agency for identification purposes.

Long-term capital gain: A gain made on the buying and selling of a capital asset held for more than one year.

Low-grade, high-yield bonds: Bonds issued by corporations who are able to obtain from the major rating agencies ratings that would attract most investors.

Margin availability: The difference between the amount of the cost and the cost of the liquidation, or sale, of an investment which can readily be converted into cash.

Market availability:

Margin call: A demand from a broker to repay part of a loan used to help purchase stock--if the value of the stock falls below a certain percentage of the outstanding loan amount.

Margin on mortgage loans: The number of percentage points the lender adds to the index rate to determine the interest rate to be charged.

Margin rate: The proportion of the total purchase price of securities that must be paid in cash.

Marginal tax rate: The tax rate applicable to the highest portion of one's taxable income.

Market fund: An investment asset held for continuing growth, so that the fund may be easily and quickly liquidated into cash.

Market-makers: Brokers who are willing to buy back a security from a customer at a certain price.

Market rate: Average rate of interest set by the major suppliers and users of credit.

Maturity: The date when the debt is due.

Maturity yield: The rate of return expressed in a percentage that will be obtained on an investment if the investment is held to maturity.

Minimum denomination: Smallest amount you can buy.

Money market assets: Investments in financial instruments such as bank certificates of deposit and short-term Treasury securities.

Money market CD: A certification of deposit purchased from a depository institution. The minimum denomination is $2,500 and the maturity or term is 26 weeks.

Money market investments: Investments that yield the market rate of interest as money market deposits accounts and money market mutual funds.

Mortgage bond: A bond secured by real estate.

Municipal bonds: Interest-bearing obligations of a state or any political subdivision of a state, such as a town, county, or city.

Mutual funds: Registered investment companies whose securities are offered to the public and whose assets are invested in a number of different securities in which the shareholders have, in effect, an undivided interest.

Mutual fund cash basis: An asset held in a mutual fund account relative to its actual purchase.

NASDAQ: The Over-the-Counter Market for investments.

Net equity: Total market value of the securities in the investor's account less any outstanding loans or fee charges on the account.

Net worth: The difference between the assets and debts (liabilities) of a person or household.

Net worth statement: A financial form that lists, as of a specific date, the financial assets and liabilities of a person or household, and shows the difference between the two as the net worth.

Noncompetitive bid: An offer to buy Treasury securities, in which the prospective purchaser does not state the rate of interest or yield that he or she is willing to accept.

NOW (Negotiable Order of Withdrawal) account: An interest bearing account on which checks may be drawn.

NYSE: The New York Stock Exchange. An investment market which trades investments each business day when the market is open for business. The NYSE is considered to be a superior trading center for investments.

One-signature account: An account owned by two or more persons arranged so that either joint owners is authorized to conduct transactions.

Open-end: Companies in which new share of the fund are sold whenever there is a request.

Opportunity cost: The benefit foregone (or opportunity lost) by using an asset in a particular venture other than its best alternative use.

Optimum value: Not always the highest rate of return, but a respectable rate of return, in view of other desirable characteristics, such as safety, liquidity, and minimum tax liability.

Option: The right to buy or sell something as a specified price within a specified period of time.

Optional negotiability: The choice of letting the owner of the certificate transfer it to another person through the proper endorsement.

Overdraft: A check written by a depositor for more money than the depositor has in his or her account.

Overdraft checking: A checking account associated with a line of credit that allows a person to write checks for more than the actual balance in the account, with a finance charge on the overdraft.

Overdrawing an account: Writing a check for more than the balance on deposit in the account.

Par value: The face value printed on common and preferred stocks and bonds. As this is meaningless for common stock, most of this stock is issued as no-par stock of one-dollar par.

Passbook savings account: A savings account in which the saver has a book to record all transactions, such as deposits, withdrawals, and interest earnings.

Passive activity: Any activity that involves the conduct of any trade or business, and in which the taxpayer does not materially participate. Any rental activity is considered a passive activity even if the taxpayer does materially participate in the activity.

Personal balance sheet: The list of assets and liabilities in an individual's investment holdings account. The difference between the two accounts is either positive or profitable, or negative or loss for the account.

P/E ratio: Price/Earnings ratio, expressed as a multiple of the price of a share of stock to the company's earnings per share.

Petition: A written request to a court or a judge asking the granting of some remedy or relief.

Point of Sale (POS): Point of sale systems allow for transfer of funds between accounts, authorization for credit, verification of checks and provision of related services at the time of purchase. POS terminals are located in some shopping areas and allow customers of participating financial institutions to effect transactions through the use of machine-readable debit cards.

Points: Additional fees that may be charged in home equity loans and are often collected at closing. A point is equal to one percent of the amount financed.

Portfolio: The aggregate of investments held by an individual or organization.

Portfolio summary: The report of activity of assets held as investments for a specified period of time.

Preferred stock: Corporate ownership that features a fixed dollar income. If the corporation has any earnings, this form of ownership has a claim on earnings and assets before the claim of common stock.

Premium bonds: Bonds selling above par.

Prime rate: Interest rate charged by commercial banks to their most credit-worthy customers. It is a minimum rate and it takes into account the customer's deposit balance and financial strength.

Principal: The total amount borrowed originally, or the face amount of the loan.

Proceeds of the policy: The total amount of the insurance policy realized or to be received by the beneficiary when the policy is paid off.

Profit taking: Securities liquidated for the purpose of realizing the amount of gain, or profit.

Project bonds: Municipal obligations, with maturities longer than one year, backed by the federal government.

Project notes: Municipal obligations, with one-year maturities, backed by the federal government.

Prospectus: A document issued by a company and filed with the Securities and Exchange Commission to describe the securities to be offered for sale and under what conditions they will be offered, as well as the prospects for company performance.

Rate: A percentage of the principal; the fixed interest that the issuer or borrower promises to pay you for using your money.

Rating organization: Firms that operate investment advisory services. The firms evaluate the relative worth of particular securities.

Real income: An individual's income in dollars adjusted for a change in the price level.

Realized gains, losses: "Realized" as used here means actual results following a period of investing of assets.

Redeem: To buy back.

Regional exchanges: Any organized securities exchange outside New York City.

Registered bond: A bond in which the owner's name is registered with the paying agent. The paying agent is a commercial bank that distributes the interest payments and repayment of principal.

Reinvestment options: An investor has the choice of withdrawing an investment for cash or for reentering the net proceeds for investing back into an investment.

Remaining liquid: Having assets in cash or in a form that can be converted to cash immediately and easily.

Repurchase agreements: Agreements by a bank or the Federal Reserve to buy back, under certain terms, securities that it originally sold to a second party.

Returned check: A check submitted by a depositor to his or her bank for payment but returned unpaid for one reason or another.

Revenue bond: Bond for which the interest and return of principal is payable from and secured by stated and expected revenues from a specific project or group of projects.

Risk: The element of the possibility of experiencing a loss for an investment.

Round lot: The general unit of trading in a security, such as 100 shares.

Savings instrument: Any contractual agreement with a financial institution in which the saver is assured of interest earnings on his or her funds.

Securities Exchange Commission (SEC): The federal agency charged with the responsibility of regulating the securities market and all publicly held investment companies.

Second mortgage: A loan specifically secured by an individual's equity in real property, which is subordinated to the equity interests of any first mortgage holder.

Secondary market: A market for buying and selling previously issued securities.

Secured bond: A bond secured by tangible assets.

Short-selling: A technique in which an investor borrows stock from a broker in the hope of selling it on the market when the price of the stock is high, then buying it back when the price has dropped, and returning it to the broker after having made a profit.

Short-term: A period of one year or less.

Signature loan: A loan granted on the basis of a borrower's credit worthiness and signature; not secured by collateral.

Simple interest: A method of calculating interest on the outstanding balance that produces a declining finance charge with each payment of the installment loan.

Sinking fund: A reserve of cash set aside annually from corporate earnings to ensure that there will be enough money to redeem bonds at maturity.

Smaller companies: Companies with small amount of business activity. Their stock price and/or their potential growth may be somewhat less than large, well established companies.

Speculative venture: An investment made despite great uncertainty in the hope of making a profit or achieving a substantial gain.

Split rate: An interest rate structure that pays regular NOW account rate on the first $2,500 and a much higher rate on the account balance above $2,500.

Statute of limitations: A law which bars suits upon valid claims after the expiration of a specified period of time.

Statutes: Laws established by the acts of a legislature.

Stock certificate: Evidence of ownership of stock in the form of a certificate, which shows, among other things, the number of shares owned, the issuing corporation, whether the stock is at par value, and the rights of the stockholder.

Stock split: When a successful company experiences its stock price at a high dollar per share value, it may offer its stock holders a stock split to reduce the per share value but also proportionately increase the per stock value. No monetary gain is thusly realized.

Stop payment: A request by a depositor to his or her bank to refuse payment on a check written by the depositor.

Strong, large companies: Companies with a history of regularly paying its stockholders dividends and the value of its stock having shown consistent and substantial growth.

Sweep: An operation in which a depository institution periodically removes funds from one account of a depositor and places such funds into a higher-yielding account for the depositor.

Tax avoidance: The use of legal means to minimize one's taxes.

T-bills: Short-term U. S. Treasury securities issued in minimum denominations of $10,000 and usually having initial maturities of three, six, or twelve months.

Tender: A form used to purchase Treasury bills.

Term: The length of time for which the principal is borrowed.

"Thrifts:" A general term for savings and loan associations, credit unions, mutual savings banks, and savings banks.

Time deposits: Funds that are deposited under agreement for a stipulated period of time.

Timing: An investor who purchases or liquidates an investment at a time which he selects as advantageous to him is using timing to his advantage.

Title: Evidence that a person is the legal owner of property.

Transactions account: Any account on which checks are written regularly to pay bills.

Transfer agent: A firm, typically a bank, that is authorized by a corporation to administer and record the transfer of its stocks or bonds between investors.

Treasury notes: Intermediate-term, coupon-bearing U. S. Treasury securities having initial maturities of from two to ten years and issued in denominations of $1,000 or more.

Treasury securities: Interest-bearing obligations of the U. S. government issued by the Treasury Department. These obligations fall into three categories--bills, notes, and bonds.

Variable annuity: An annuity contract providing lifetime retirement payments that vary in amount with the results of investment in a separate account portfolio.

Variable rate: An interest rate that changes periodically in relation to an index. Payments may increase or decrease accordingly.

Variable rate certificate: A savings certificate on which the rate of interest payable changes, depending on the term for which the money is pledged.

Vendors: Companies that sell.

Volatility: A measure of the rapidity with which a security changes in value as compared to the market generally.

Yield (or rate of return): Measurement of the profitability of an investment; it is usually per year on the amount invested; often referred to as return on investment.

Zero coupon bond: A bond that pays no interest. It is sold at a deep discount at the time of issuance; thus the buyer's gain is the difference between the discount price and the face value of the bond collected at maturity.

This Glossary, or alphabetized list of definitions for Advanced Investors, is commonly used by professionals in the exacting field of outlines and limits. The author has used the list over the years and has experienced conformity, understanding and unanimity among other leaders of the profession.

INDEX

A

INDEX